Passport to Latin America and Canada

Grade 5 Teacher's Edition

Contents

Carol Aronin, *Social Studies Consultant;* Syosset, New York

Michael A. Colucci, *Social Studies Consultant, Historian;* Valley Cottage, New York

Editorial Offices: Glenview, Illinois • Parsippany, New Jersey • New York, New York

Sales Offices: Parsippany, New Jersey • Duluth, Georgia • Glenview, Illinois •
Coppell, Texas • Ontario, California • Mesa, Arizona

ISBN: 0-328-05597-2

How to Use This Book

★ ★

Passport to Latin America and Canada brings students insight into the histories of Latin America and Canada, extending the coverage in the Grade 5 text, *The United States*, of the Scott Foresman Social Studies program. Each unit covers the same time period as the corresponding unit in *The United States*. However, because information is presented in chronological order, this book could be used with any U.S. history textbook of similar scope. Thus, students can place the information on Canada and Latin America in the context of what they've learned about the United States.

With support from this Teacher's Guide, *Passport* provides strong content, accessibility, motivation, and accountability. The content covers the key social studies strands, makes use of primary source material, and provides depth of coverage through biographies and other features. Every unit includes a targeted reading comprehension skill supported by graphic organizers, and leveled practice and ESL support are also given. Each lesson begins with You Are There, a dramatic reading that sets the stage for the content and lets students experience events from a personal perspective. For assessment, there are built-in lesson and unit reviews that focus on targeted skills and main ideas.

In addition, every unit contains a series of Document-Based Questions (DBQs). These require students to analyze various types of documents—maps, photographs, text, charts, tables, and so on—and use them to answer history-related questions. The even-numbered units each contain six DBQs plus a DBQ Essay page, from which students write on a topic that relates to all of the DBQs from that unit. For the odd-numbered units, you will find an essay suggestion in the Teacher's Guide. The odd-numbered units each contain six DBQs, including one DBQ-support page that offers students tips on analyzing a specific type of document.

Pages 3 and 4 of this book contain samples of the DBQ-support pages. These will help familiarize you with the concept. Page 5 provides a sheet you can copy and give to students to assist them in writing their DBQ essays. A similar page in each unit of the Teacher's Guide provides greater detail, answers to DBQs, alternative organizers, and other information that will help you with each essay. Page 6 provides another sheet you can copy, the DBQ Record Sheet, which students can use to record their answers to DBQs in each unit; this will also be helpful to them in writing their essays.

Maps

An elevation map shows the elevation, or height, of land in different places. Elevation is measured in feet or meters above sea level. Sea level is the height of the surface of the ocean when it is halfway between high tide and low tide.

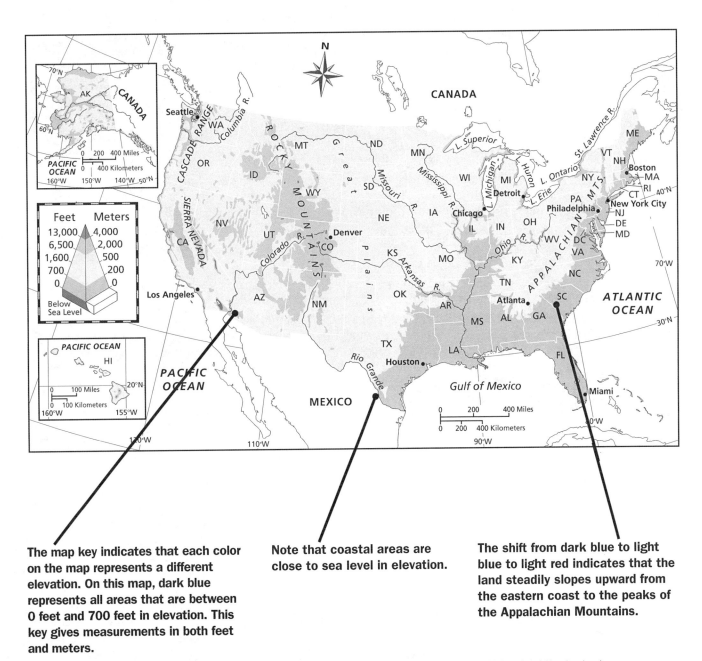

The map key indicates that each color on the map represents a different elevation. On this map, dark blue represents all areas that are between 0 feet and 700 feet in elevation. This key gives measurements in both feet and meters.

Note that coastal areas are close to sea level in elevation.

The shift from dark blue to light blue to light red indicates that the land steadily slopes upward from the eastern coast to the peaks of the Appalachian Mountains.

▶ Look at the major rivers in the central part of the United States (the Ohio, the Mississippi, the Missouri, and the Arkansas). Look at the elevation information in the map.

DOCUMENT-BASED QUESTION *Based on the information provided by this map, which direction would you conclude these rivers flow? How does the information in the map provide evidence to support your conclusion?*

Text

Text documents are an excellent source of information. Readers who examine a document carefully are often able to draw information from it beyond its literal content. Looking at the language and format of a document can help the reader evaluate the meaning of the text.

By asking this question, the writer makes a personal connection between the reader and the topic.

Including a quotation adds weight to the writing. A quotation from a respected national leader such as Theodore Roosevelt provides additional support for the writer's viewpoint.

Our National Parks

Have you ever hiked or camped in a park? Creating parks is one way to help protect the environment. National parks are parks that are protected by the federal government. The first national park in the United States was Yellowstone National Park, established in 1872. Congress created Yellowstone park "for the benefit and enjoyment of the people."

Since then, people of all ages have worked to create new parks around the country. Theodore Roosevelt, president from 1901 to 1909, helped create several national parks. Read what he said about protecting the Grand Canyon as a national park:

> "Leave it as it is. You cannot improve on it. . . . what you can do is to keep it for your children, your children's children, and for all who come after you."

Today, there are more than 50 national parks from Maine to Hawaii, covering more than 50 million acres. Each park has features that make it special. In Yellowstone National Park, you might see rare animals such as grizzly bears, mountain lions, and gray wolves. In Alaska's Denali National Park you can look up at Mount McKinley, the highest peak in North America. Explore the world's longest cave system at Mammoth Cave National Park in Kentucky. Or visit Florida's Everglades National Park to see alligators, manatees, and bottle-nosed dolphins.

The writer includes facts about the national park system.

By describing specific features of several parks, the writer makes each park seem unique and valuable.

▶ Use the document and tips above to answer this question:

DOCUMENT-BASED QUESTION *Does the writer believe it is good for America to have a national park system? Provide two or more examples from the document that support your answer.*

Essay

Plan and Prewrite

Review the DBQ documents and questions from the unit and review your answers from your DBQ Record Sheet. How does each document relate to the topic of the essay? How can you use each document to support what you want to say? Remember that the unit provides the historical context for your essay.

A graphic organizer may help you organize your thoughts for your essay. You might create a chart like the one below to record your thoughts about each document.

Cause: Unfair Land Distribution		
Document		
How It Relates to Topic		
Notes		

You could also use other graphic organizers with which you are familiar.

Evaluate and Revise

After you have completed your first draft, use the following checklist to evaluate what you have written:

☐ Have I used information from the documents to draw my conclusion?

☐ Have I shown how information or ideas from each document are related to the topic?

☐ Have I included my own thoughts in the essay?

☐ Have I avoided simply summarizing the documents?

☐ Is my point clearly stated and explained?

☐ Is my essay logically organized?

☐ Do I use appropriate details to support my topic sentences?

☐ Have I avoided including statements that are unrelated to the topic?

Proofread After they have edited their essays for content, remind students to use a standard proofreading checklist to look for errors in spelling, grammar, and mechanics. Then have them write and submit the final drafts of their essays.

Score the Essay You may wish to use the rubric at right to score students' essays. If you have emphasized particular thinking or writing strategies during the study of a unit, you may wish to modify the rubric to include those skills.

Scoring Rubric
Document-Based Essay

4	• Shows superior understanding of the topic. • Relates details from the documents to the topic. • Includes numerous insights (conclusions, inferences) that are well explained and supported by the documents. • Includes no factual or mechanical errors.
3	• Shows reasonable understanding of the topic. • Relates most of the details from the documents to the topic. • Includes some insights (conclusions, inferences) that are clear and for the most part supported by the documents. • Includes very few factual or mechanical errors.
2	• Shows minimal understanding of the topic. • Attempts to relate some details from the documents to the topic. • Includes details, quotes, or paraphrasing from the documents, but no insights (conclusions, inferences) into the topic. • Includes a number of factual or mechanical errors.
1	• Shows little or no understanding of the topic. • Does not attempt to relate details from the documents to the topic. • Includes only vague references, if any, to content of the documents. • Includes many factual or mechanical errors.
0	• Uses no accurate data, or response is totally unrelated to the topic. • Is either illegible or incoherent, and no sense can be made of the response. • Paper is blank.

Record Sheet

Use this Record Sheet to record your answers to the Document-Based Questions in each unit.

UNIT _____

DBQ from page _____

_____

_____

_____

DBQ from page _____

_____

_____

_____

DBQ from page _____

_____

_____

_____

DBQ from page _____

_____

_____

_____

DBQ from page _____

_____

_____

_____

DBQ from page _____

_____

_____

_____

Early Americans, North and South

Unit Overview

The physical geography of regions in North and South America affected the lives of the early people who settled there. People in North America's Arctic region relied on the harpoon for whale hunting; eastern settlers farmed; people in the plains followed the buffalo. Central Americans also farmed. Diverse cultures arose in South America. Many were nomadic, but in the Andes region, some built cities and raised crops.

Draw a K-W-L chart on the board and label it *North America*. Also display a map of this region. Remind students that Canada is part of North America, as are the United States, Mexico, and Central America. Ask students to tell you what they know about the physical geography and natural resources of North America. Remind students that natural resources are things found in nature that people can use. Record students' responses in the *K* column. Ask what they know about the early peoples who settled in North America. Record their responses in the *K* column. Then ask them what questions they have about the physical geography of Canada, the early people of Canada, and how geography affected people's lives. Record students' questions in the *W* column of the chart. As students study the unit, record what they learn in the *L* column. Make a second K-W-L chart and label it *Latin America*. Explain that Latin America includes South America and parts of North America. (The map on p. 7 of the PE may help clarify this.) Display a map of these regions. Repeat the procedure described above to complete the chart on Latin America.

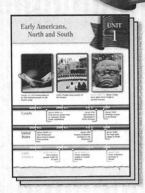

Pupil Edition page 1

 SOCIAL STUDIES
Background

About Horses

- Tell students that scientists have found fossils that indicate horses originated mainly in North America. The animals then crossed land bridges to Eurasia and South America. However, these early horses vanished from the Americas about 10,000 years ago. Early settlers in the Americas had to travel by foot. Horses eventually became domesticated in Europe and Asia, and European settlers brought horses to North America. The introduction of the horse significantly changed the lives of native peoples. They could now travel faster and farther and use the horses to carry loads and help with farm work.

About Caral

- Explain to students that even though Caral, Peru, sits about 14 miles from the coast, fish bones and mollusk shells have been found there. The people of Caral grew squash and beans. They traded these crops for fish and mollusks from people living along the coast.

 **Additional Information**

⚠️ *To establish guidelines for your students' safe and responsible use of the Internet, use the Scott Foresman Internet Guide.*

Internet Links

To find out more about

- The Inuit, visit **www.itk.ca** key word *history*
- Caral, visit **www.smithsonianmag.si.edu** key word *Caral*
- Events in the United States at this time, visit **www.sfsocialstudies.com**

Pupil Edition pages 2–5

Objectives

- Describe how glaciers shaped the physical environment of Canada.
- Identify technology developed by early Canadians.
- Explain how early people used Canada's natural resources to satisfy their wants and needs.

Vocabulary

First Nations, p. 4; **Three Sisters,** p. 4; **nomad,** p. 5

Quick Teaching Plan

If time is short, have pairs or groups of students label maps of Canada.

- As they read the lesson independently, have students mark the map to show the geographic regions described in the lesson.
- Have students create a map key and label the map to show where early people lived and what natural resources they used.

Early Life in Canada

1 Introduce and Motivate

Preview To activate prior knowledge, ask students to brainstorm about landforms that are found in their area. Then ask them to describe the climate in the region. Have students discuss both positive and negative ways that landforms and climate affect how they live. Tell students that as they read Lesson 1, they will learn how landforms and climate affected the first people who settled in North America.

2 Teach and Discuss

Quick Summary The first people to live in Canada depended on natural resources. Some developed harpoons to hunt whales. Some lived a nomadic existence hunting buffalo. Others became farmers, using the rich soil to grow crops.

The Land of Canada   p. 3

- **Do you think life was more difficult for people after mammoths began to die out?** Possible answers: Yes; people had to start hunting smaller animals, so they would have had to hunt more often to get enough food. No; smaller animals would be easier to hunt. **Hypothesize**

✔ **REVIEW ANSWER** Similar: Both regions once had steep mountains, but glaciers wore the peaks away. Different: In the Appalachian region, glaciers wore the mountains into the low, rounded Appalachian Mountains. In the Canadian Shield, the glaciers left a rocky, bowl-shaped landscape. **Compare and Contrast**

People of the North and East   p. 4

- **Why were the Iroquois able to develop a strong democratic government?** Possible answer: Moving from place to place took time and probably disrupted the community. Because the Iroquois did not have to move, they developed a close community and could devote more time to developing government. **Make Inferences**

✔ **REVIEW ANSWER** People in the northeast hunted with bows and arrows, traps, and snares. They lived in small groups and moved frequently. They also gathered fruits, nuts, and roots. People in the southeast planted seeds and raised corn, beans, and squash. They lived in one place and developed a strong, democratic government. **Summarize**

People of the West pp. 4–5

- **How do you think life changed for the Plains Indians after Europeans brought horses to Canada?** Possible answers: They could travel faster. Hunting would be easier. **Make Inferences**

✓ **REVIEW ANSWER** The First Nations of the Plains followed buffalo herds and moved from place to place. They used a device called a travois to move their belongings. **Summarize**

3 Close and Assess

Summarize the Lesson Have students work in groups to make an expanded time line of events from the lesson. Ask students to write their time lines on the board.

✓ Lesson 1 REVIEW

1. **Summarize**

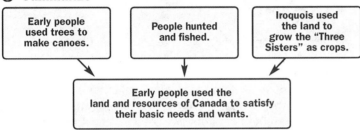

| Early people used trees to make canoes. | People hunted and fished. | Iroquois used the land to grow the "Three Sisters" as crops. |

Early people used the land and resources of Canada to satisfy their basic needs and wants.

2. As mammoths became scarce, people depended on smaller game as a source of food.

3. Rounded Appalachian Mountains, bowl-shaped landscape lakes of the Canadian Shield, and glacial deposits show glaciers once moved across the land.

4. Whaling harpoons made it easier to survive in the Arctic.

5. **Critical Thinking: *Compare and Contrast*** The First Nations of the Plains moved frequently to find good hunting; the First Nations in southeast Canada grew crops, stayed in one place, and developed a close community. The environments and the natural resources of the areas in which these groups lived influenced the way they lived.

Link to ⟳⟳ Writing Students should include descriptions and facts about the Inuit that they learned from their Internet research. Suggest they discuss Inuit contributions to Canadian culture.

C SOCIAL STUDIES STRAND
Culture

- The Iroquois not only planted the crops known as the Three Sisters together, they also ate the corn, beans, and squash together. This combination of foods provided important nutritional benefits, because each type of food supplies nutrients that the others lack.

- Iroquois women were primarily responsible for the planting, tending, and harvesting of the Three Sisters, though men assisted in clearing the land before planting. Women used digging sticks and hoes to plant the crops.

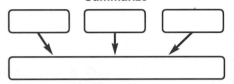
READING STRATEGY
Summarize

In the Lesson Review, students complete a graphic organizer like the one below. You may want to provide students with a copy of Transparency 6 to complete as they read the lesson.

Summarize

MEETING INDIVIDUAL NEEDS
Leveled Practice

Compare and Contrast Ways of Life Have students compare how people lived in western Canada and in northern Canada.

Easy Ask students to choose the geographic region of either western Canada or northern Canada. Have them write a sentence about how early people there lived. **Reteach**

On-Level Have students create Venn diagrams to compare and contrast how people lived in these two geographic regions. **Extend**

Challenge Have groups of students use library resources to research the lives of early people in either western Canada or northern Canada. **Enrich**

CURRICULUM CONNECTION
Science

Produce a Glacier Quiz Show

- Have students use the Internet or other library resources to answer the following questions: *How do glaciers form? How do glaciers move? What is inside a glacier? Where can glaciers be found today?*

- Ask students to write questions based on the information they find.

- Have students produce a quiz show about glaciers. One student can be the host and others can be contestants. Have the host read the questions students wrote. The first contestant to correctly answer each question will score a point.

LESSON 2

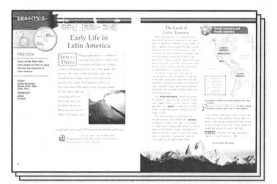

Pupil Edition pages 6–9

Objectives
- Describe how the movement of geological plates has shaped the landscape of Latin America.
- Explain how early peoples in Latin America used natural resources to satisfy their basic needs and wants.
- Describe how Olmec ideas and ways of life were spread in Latin America.

Vocabulary

plates, p. 7; **pampas,** p. 7

Quick Teaching Plan

If time is short, have students create a chart of the characteristics of early life in Latin America.

- Have students make a three-column chart with the heading *Early Life in Latin America.*
- Ask students to record details from each of the three lesson sections. Students may include details from photographs or maps that help them understand the main point of the lesson.

Early Life in Latin America

1 Introduce and Motivate

Preview To activate prior knowledge, ask students to name different kinds of tools people use for working with natural resources or their environments (fishing nets, snow shovels, and so on). Ask what tool the Inuit used for hunting (harpoon). Tell students that as they read Lesson 2, they will learn of some tools early people in Latin America used to help them live in their environments.

2 Teach and Discuss

Quick Summary The land regions of South America have mountains, plains, and highlands. The early people of Latin America were nomads, but evidence of later farming communities has been found in both Central and South America. The Olmec of Central America are considered the first great civilization in the Americas.

The Land of Latin America   p. 7

- **How have volcanoes affected the landscape of Central America?** Lava from volcanoes hardened in layers and formed mountains. **Cause and Effect**

✓ **REVIEW ANSWER** The western coast is a high, rugged, mountainous area. The central plains have swamps, forests, pampas, and large rivers. The eastern highlands have rocky plateaus, domes, and hills. ⊙ **Summarize**

Early Peoples   p. 8

- **What evidence suggests that the people of Monte Verde were hunters?** Spears, tools made of bone, and shelters covered with animal hide have been found there. **Make Inferences**

✓ **REVIEW ANSWER** People could live in one place and build permanent homes and settlements. They had more time to do other things, such as weaving, basket making, and ceramic work. **Main Idea and Details**

The Olmec   p. 9

- **Name one example that shows that the Olmec influenced the Aztec culture.** The Aztec calendar was similar to the Olmec calendar. **Apply Information**

✓ **REVIEW ANSWER** The Olmec made advances in architecture and art and developed a calendar. They also built large buildings, pyramids, plazas, and temples. ⊙ **Summarize**

3 Close and Assess

Summarize the Lesson Display a map of Central and South America. Have students attach sticky notes with the labels *Andes Mountains, Monte Verde,* and *Caral* to the appropriate places on the map. Have them point out where the Olmec civilization thrived and name examples of that culture's achievements.

✓ Lesson 2 REVIEW

1. ⊙ **Summarize**

| Early people made tools from bone and rock. | Early people used animal hides on their shelters. | Early people used the land to grow crops. |

↓ ↓ ↙

Early people used the land and resources of Latin America to satisfy their basic needs and wants.

2. The Andes began forming millions of years ago when two of Earth's plates collided, causing the Andes to rise and form.

3. Archaeologists found remains of a small camp with artifacts such as digging sticks, spears, and tools made of bone, tusk, and stone. They also found pieces of shelters covered with animal hide.

4. When food sources became scarce, people moved to find more plants and animals.

5. Critical Thinking: *Cause and Effect* Life would have been more comfortable because the Olmec built large buildings and plazas. People would have enjoyed Olmec artwork such as jewelry, masks, and giant stone heads. The Olmec also influenced later cultures—the Aztec calendar was similar to the Olmec calendar.

Link to ∞ Science Students should first list the common uses of the tools. Although the nontraditional uses they come up with can be creative, they should also be somewhat logical.

Map Adventure

1. The Inuit lived in the Arctic region in the far north of North America. This region was covered in glaciers.

2. The Iroquois lived in a region of rounded, rolling mountains with rich soil, while the Olmec lived in a steep, mountainous region with volcanoes. The Iroquois became farmers because of the rich soil that was available. The Olmec built buildings and created artwork using stone that must have been abundant in their mountainous region.

3. Possible answer: The people at Caral used the stones around them to make buildings; people used fishing nets to catch food; people adapted the land to their needs by building irrigation canals.

SOCIAL STUDIES STRAND
Geography

Mental Mapping Have students draw an outline map of South America from memory. Have them create a map key for steep mountains, low mountains and hills, and flat plains. Have them label the map to show the geographic regions of the continent.

READING STRATEGY
Summarize

In the Lesson Review, students complete a graphic organizer like the one below. You may want to provide students with a copy of Transparency 6 to complete as they read the lesson.

Summarize

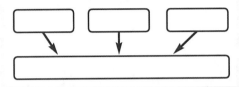

EXTEND LANGUAGE
ESL Support

Examine Suffixes Explain to students that noun suffixes *-er* and *-ist* can be used to tell about a person's job.

Beginning Explain that the suffix *-er* means "one who" and the suffix *-ist* means "one who practices." Write *archaeologist, artist, farmer,* and *hunter* on the board. Have students identify the suffix in each word. Discuss the meanings of the root words and the words with the suffixes added.

Intermediate Give students the following root words: *teach, art, farm,* and *biology.* Then have students use the suffixes *-er* and *-ist* to form words that tell about a person's job. Remind students that words that end in *y* drop the *y* before adding *-ist.*

Advanced Have students look through Unit 1 to find words with suffixes *-er* and *-ist* that tell about people's jobs (*archaeologist, artist, farmer, hunter*). Then tell students that other words in the unit use the suffixes *-ous, -al,* and *-ology* (*mountainous, natural, technology*). Have students look up the meanings of these suffixes and then use the suffixes to form words. Ask students to define the words they form.

Write the Essay

Plan and Prewrite

You may wish to have students use the documents in this unit to write an essay about how early peoples in the Americas used natural resources. Discuss the topic and share with students the rubric that will be used to score their essays (see TE p. 13). Have students review the documents and the answers they recorded on their DBQ record sheets.

Page 4, photo: The Inuit lived where snow was abundant, so they built their shelters from snow and ice.

Page 4, diagram: The beans climbed the cornstalks. The squash kept the weeds away from the corn and beans. The beans provided nitrogen to the soil.

Page 5, illustration: The travois was made of two poles tied together. You can see that it was small because it was pulled by a dog. The Plains Indians may have used travois because they were easy to make with available resources.

Page 7, map: Mexico is a North American country that is part of Latin America.

Page 8, photo: Possible answer: They might have dug for roots or insects.

Page 11, excerpt:
- They wove cloth from bark; used roots and branches to make baskets, dishes, and cooking pots; made canoes from the trunk; used fibers for fishing nets and traps; made masks from the inner bark; and used the dried wood for tinder.
- They were not afraid of letting the fires go out because they could easily start a new fire.
- Students may mention items such as war canoes or dancing masks, or that the Cree thought that cedar was the "greatest gift."

Discuss Before students begin planning their essays, you may wish to have a class discussion to stimulate students' thinking. Ask students to identify the various natural resources in the documents. Remind students that the unit provides the historical context for their responses.

Use a Graphic Organizer Remind students that a prewriting tool such as a graphic organizer will help them write a better essay. Model on the board a T-chart.

Suggest that students complete the graphic organizer with details that tell specific ways in which early people used natural resources. Remind students that their essays should not simply list natural resources but should also explain why these resources were important to people.

Tell students they may use other kinds of organizers as long as the organizers are suited to the topic. Once students complete their prewriting, have them write first drafts of their essays.

Content Tips Have students reread the excerpt on PE p. 11. Suggest that students' essays speculate about the important role "a small handful of earth and a tiny plant" came to play in Cree society.

Natural Resources	Uses

Evaluate and Revise

Check Content Once students have completed their first drafts, provide the following checklist to assist them in evaluating what they have written:

- ❑ Have I used information from the documents to draw my conclusion?
- ❑ Have I shown how information or ideas from each document are related to the topic?
- ❑ Have I included my own thoughts in the essay?
- ❑ Have I avoided simply summarizing the documents?
- ❑ Is my point clearly stated and explained?
- ❑ Is my essay logically organized?
- ❑ Do I use appropriate details to support my topic sentences?
- ❑ Have I avoided including statements that are unrelated to the topic?

Proofread After they have edited their essays for content, remind students to use a standard proofreading checklist to look for errors in spelling, grammar, and mechanics. Then have them write and submit the final drafts of their essays.

Score the Essay You may wish to use the rubric at right to score students' essays. If you have emphasized particular thinking or writing strategies during the study of Unit 1, you may wish to modify the rubric to include those skills.

Scoring Rubric
Unit 1 Document-Based Essay

4
- Shows superior understanding of the topic.
- Relates each document to the topic of natural resources.
- Includes numerous insights (conclusions, inferences) that are well explained and supported by the documents.
- Includes no factual or mechanical errors.

3
- Shows reasonable understanding of the topic.
- Relates most of the details from documents to the topic of natural resources.
- Includes some insights (conclusions, inferences) that are clear and for the most part supported by the documents.
- Includes very few factual or mechanical errors.

2
- Shows minimal understanding of the topic.
- Attempts to relate some details from the documents to the topic of natural resources.
- Includes details, quotes, or paraphrasing, but no insights (conclusions, inferences) into the topic.
- Includes a number of factual or mechanical errors.

1
- Shows little or no understanding of the topic.
- Does not attempt to relate details from the documents to the topic of natural resources.
- Includes only vague references, if any, to content of the documents.
- Includes many factual or mechanical errors.

0
- Uses no accurate data, or response is totally unrelated to the topic.
- Is either illegible or incoherent, and no sense can be made of the response.
- Paper is blank.

Pupil Edition page 12

Vocabulary and Places

Sample answers:

1. The Appalachian region is an area in eastern Canada that glaciers changed from high, steep mountains to low, rounded mountains.

2. The First Nations, including the Inuit, are the descendants of Canada's earliest peoples.

3. Pampas are the prairies in the central plains of South America.

4. Monte Verde is a place in Chile where archaeologists discovered the remains of a camp from more than 12,000 years ago. The artifacts found there show how early people lived in that area.

5. Caral is the oldest known city in the Americas.

Facts and Main Ideas

Sample answers:

1. The ancient people of Monte Verde made tools from bone, tusk, and stone.

2. **Main Idea** Early peoples in Latin America hunted animals and gathered plants in the area for food. They used the land to grow maize, chilies, and guava. They used stone and other materials to make tools.

3. The Woodland First Nations hunted with bows and arrows, traps, and snares.

4. **Main Idea** Early peoples in Canada hunted animals and gathered food from the plants in the area. Some used the rich soil to grow crops. They used trees and other natural materials to make canoes, tools, and other objects.

5. **Critical Thinking:** *Apply Information* The mountain ranges would be steeper. The landscapes would not be as rocky or carved out, and lakes would not have been formed.

Write About History

1. Students' riddles should include accurate clues that describe the place or land region.

2. Students' narratives might mention geographical features and tools used. Students should provide reasons why they do or do not like aspects of their way of life.

3. Students' guidebook entries should include three or more details. They should describe both the physical geography and the area's modern features.

Read on Your Own

The Inuit of Canada, by Danielle Corriveau (Lerner Publications Company, ISBN 0-822-54850-X, 2001) **Easy**

The Iroquois, edited by Petra Press (Compass Point Books, ISBN 0-756-50080-X, 2001) **Easy**

Eyewitness: Aztec, Inca & Maya, by Elizabeth Baquedano (DK Publishing, ISBN 0-789-46115-3, 2000) **On-Level**

Glaciers, by Roy A. Gallant (Franklin Watts, ISBN 0-531-20390-5, 1999) **On-Level**

Myths of Pre-Columbian America, by Anita Dalal (Raintree/Steck Vaughn, ISBN 0-739-83193-3, 2002) **Challenge**

Secret of the Andes, by Ann Nolan Clark (Viking Press, ISBN 0-140-30926-8, 1976) **Challenge** *Newbery Medal winner*

Connections Across Continents

Unit Overview

European exploration escalated in the 1500s and 1600s. After the Inca civil war, Spanish explorer Francisco Pizarro easily conquered the Inca Empire. The Portuguese explored Brazil and enslaved the native peoples. A mixed culture developed among the *mestizos,* people of native and European blood. While English and Dutch colonists were settling into what would become the United States, English and French explorers arrived in Canada and began a system of commerce in which they traded with the native peoples.

Pupil Edition page 13

Draw a K-W-L chart on the board and label it *European Exploration in the Americas.* Ask students to tell you what they know about European explorers and settlers who came to the Americas after Columbus. Record students' responses in the *K* column. Guide the discussion by reminding students of what they know about the native peoples who occupied the area before Europeans arrived. Then ask what questions students have about the European explorers who came to Canada and Latin America. Record students' questions in the *W* column of the chart. As students study the unit, record in the *L* column any answers they learn.

SOCIAL STUDIES
Background

About the Quipu

- The Inca had no system of writing. They did, however, have the *quipu.* This device recorded information on colored, knotted strings. Professional quipu keepers used their quipus to record Inca history, poems, and data. They shared a code, so one quipu keeper could "read" the quipus of others. When the last quipu keeper died after the Spanish conquest, the knowledge of how to read the quipus disappeared for hundreds of years. It was not until the 1920s that a historian deciphered the Inca system of recording numbers on the quipu.

About the Founding of Montreal

- Tell students that in 1642 a group of French missionaries set out to create a model Catholic community in what is now Montreal. Their goal was to convert the native peoples in the area. The missionaries had some success and built the Sulpician Seminary, but frequent attacks on the settlement by the Iroquois ended hopes of a missionary community.

Additional Information

⚠️ *To establish guidelines for your students' safe and responsible use of the Internet, use the Scott Foresman Internet Guide.*

Internet Links

To find out more about

- The Inca Empire, visit **www.pbs.org** key words *Atahualpa, Cuzco*
- French explorers, visit **www.get2knowcanada.ca** key words *Jacques Cartier*
- Events in the United States at this time, visit **www.sfsocialstudies.com**

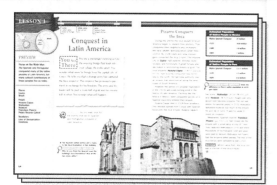

Pupil Edition pages 14–17

Objectives

- Explain how diseases brought by the Spanish changed life in Peru.
- Describe how the Portuguese used natural and human resources to create wealth in Portuguese Brazil.
- Identify how the native peoples of Latin America have contributed to the cultures of their nations.

Vocabulary

Line of Demarcation, p. 16;
mestizos, p. 16

Quick Teaching Plan

If time is short, have students create a Venn diagram to compare and contrast the changes Europeans brought to the Inca Empire and to Brazil.

- Draw a Venn diagram on the board. Label the left circle *How the Inca Empire Changed* and the right circle *How Brazil Changed.* Explain that students will record similarities in the middle, where the circles intersect.
- Have students read independently and add events to the diagram.

Conquest in Latin America

1 Introduce and Motivate

Preview To activate prior knowledge, ask students to suppose that a teacher from another school came to their classroom. The new teacher spoke a different language and wanted the class to follow new rules. Discuss with students how things would change in the classroom. Tell students that in Lesson 1 they will learn about the impact Europeans had on the life of native peoples in Latin America.

2 Teach and Discuss

Quick Summary Spanish explorers arrived in Latin America in the 1500s. They conquered the Inca Empire. At the same time, Portuguese explorers conquered Brazil and enslaved the native peoples. Spain and Portugal agreed that Spain would rule western South America and Portugal would rule eastern South America. Over time, many Europeans and native peoples married, forming a mixed culture.

Pizarro Conquers the Inca   p. 15

- **What do you think might have happened if Huayna Capac had not died? Why?** Possible answers: The Inca would have defeated the Spanish because Huayna Capac would have proved an able conqueror. The Spanish still probably would have won, but it would have taken them longer because the empire would not have been weakened by civil war. **Hypothesize**

✓ **REVIEW ANSWER** The Inca civil war happened first.
Sequence

The Portuguese in Brazil   p. 16

- **Why do you think Portugal and Spain accepted the Line of Demarcation?** Possible answer: The two countries did not want to fight over land. **Draw Conclusions**

✓ **REVIEW ANSWER** Cabral claimed Brazil after Spain and Portugal agreed on the Line of Demarcation. **Sequence**

The Contributions of Native Peoples   pp. 16–17

- **Why do you think many Mexicans follow some of the customs and traditions of their ancestors?** Possible answers: It allows them to honor the history of their people. The old ways still work. **Hypothesize**

✓ **REVIEW ANSWER** Mestizos arose. **Sequence**

3 Close and Assess

Summarize the Lesson Divide students into two groups. Have one group describe life in Cuzco after the Spanish conquest from a Spanish explorer's point of view. Have the other group describe the same time from an Inca's point of view. Repeat the activity assigning one group the point of view of a Portuguese settler and the other that of a Tupi after the Portuguese conquest of Brazil.

✓ Lesson 1 REVIEW

1. **⊙ Sequence**
   1528–1532 Inca civil war
   1532 Pizarro's army captures Atahualpa and kills thousands of his followers

2. Smallpox helped make the Inca too weak to resist invasion. It killed their emperor, which led to civil war.

3. The Portuguese used soil as a natural resource to grow sugar cane. They used the Tupi people as human resources for working on sugar plantations.

4. Some Mexicans today speak modern forms of the Maya language or the Aztec language, Náhuatl. In Peru, native peoples practice Inca farming methods. People eat potatoes, an Inca crop.

5. **Critical Thinking:** *Compare and Contrast* The Portuguese conquest of Brazil was different because Brazil did not have any wealthy empires. Instead of conquering native peoples who had material wealth, the Portuguese made use of natural and human resources to acquire wealth.

Link to ⛓ Writing Encourage students to include details such as the Inca civil war, the arrival of Pizarro, and the defeat of Atahualpa.

C SOCIAL STUDIES STRAND
Culture

The Potato in Different Cultures

Share the following information with students:

- When Spaniards first brought the potato to Europe from South America, it was slow to catch on. The leaves of a potato plant are poisonous, and many people believed the whole plant was dangerous.

- Frederick the Great, the ruler of Prussia, ordered people to plant and eat potatoes. King William of Germany distributed potatoes throughout his country with instructions about how to grow them.

- Antoine August Parmentier is credited with popularizing the potato in France in the 1700s. He had been a prisoner of war in Prussia and ate potatoes in jail. When he was released, he convinced the king and queen of France to support the potato.

- In time, the potato gained acceptance and use throughout Europe. Today, the potato is commonly used in the cuisine of all European cultures. Have students discuss ways the introduction of a new kind of food might change life in a region.

READING STRATEGY
Sequence

In the Lesson Review, students complete a graphic organizer like the one below. You may want to provide students with a copy of Transparency 11 to complete as they read the lesson.

Sequence

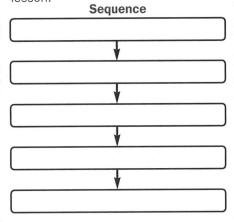

MEETING INDIVIDUAL NEEDS
Leveled Practice

Present a News Story Students give short presentations that describe how the Portuguese affected the environment and society of Brazil.

Easy Students can relate the basic facts, including how the Portuguese began planting sugar cane and enslaved Tupi to work on the plantations. **Reteach**

On-Level Students can create a news report on the topic, including a discussion about how Tupi society was largely destroyed. One student could act as a Tupi Indian and explain what life was like after the arrival of the Portuguese. **Extend**

Challenge Have students find a reference book or Internet article and read more about the Portuguese conquest of Brazil. Have one group of students play the part of reporters and another group play the parts of Cabral, Portuguese settlers, and Tupi Indians. Have the "reporters" interview the different players in the story. Encourage them to give detailed answers and to present differing points of view. **Enrich**

Pupil Edition pages 18–21

Objectives

- Identify how Europeans used the natural resources of Canada.
- Describe the economic system based on the exchange of goods between Native Americans and Europeans.
- Explain how supply and demand and the market for beaver pelts led to the development of the fur trade in Canada.

Vocabulary

voyageurs, p. 20; **Métis,** p. 20

Quick Teaching Plan

If time is short, have students prepare an outline to complete as they read the lesson.

- Have students write the headings *Events* and *People* for Roman numerals I and II.
- Ask students to complete the outline by recording details about significant events and people from each section as they read.

Coexistence in Canada

1 Introduce and Motivate

Preview To activate prior knowledge, ask students if they have ever traded items with a friend or sibling. Remind students that trading means an exchange of items that both parties want or need. Tell them that trade became an important part of the history of Canada. Students will learn in Lesson 2 about trade between Europeans and the native peoples of Canada.

> **You Are There** Point out to students that John Cabot hoped that he would find a shorter route to Asia. Ask students what John Cabot may have hoped to find during his voyage on the *Matthew.*

2 Teach and Discuss

Quick Summary When English and French explorers reached Canada, they discovered a wealth of natural resources, especially fish and fur. Soon a system of trade was set up between the Native Americans and Europeans. This trade eventually led to the growth of cities such as Quebec and Montreal.

Cabot and Cartier Claim Canada p. 19

- **Why do you think Cartier chose the Iroquois word for "village" when he named the land?** Possible answers: Cartier wanted to respect the people who had long lived in the region. He may have thought the land was like a village where people from different cultures could live together. **Make Inferences**

✓ **REVIEW ANSWER** Cartier traded with the Micmac and other Native American groups after he landed in eastern Canada. He also claimed the land for France. ⊙ **Sequence**

The Fur Trade pp. 20–21

- **What might have happened to the fur trade if the supply of beaver furs increased dramatically?** If the supply had increased, the price people were willing to pay for the fur would likely have gone down. **Draw Conclusions**

✓ **REVIEW ANSWER** Trade generally occurred first. ⊙ **Sequence**

3 Close and Assess

Summarize the Lesson Have students work in groups to prepare skits about the following events: Jacques Cartier meeting the Micmac people; a Native American trading furs for tools and cloth. Allow time for the groups to act out their skits for the class. Discuss with them the problems each individual or group represented in the skits may have encountered, such as language differences.

✓ Lesson 2 REVIEW

1. ⦿ **Sequence**

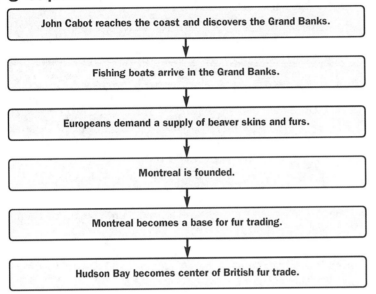

2. European traders could eat or trade the fish; they could sell beaver fur in Europe.

3. Europeans and Native Americans exchanged goods. The Europeans traded metal goods in exchange for furs from the Native Americans.

4. Beavers had been nearly killed off in Europe, but there was still a great demand for beaver fur. There was enough demand that when Europeans found a new supply in North America, they could make money by trading for furs with Native Americans and sending the furs back to Europe.

5. **Critical Thinking:** *Make Decisions* Answers will vary. Reasons to support the fur trade may include economic benefits and building good relationships with Native Americans. Reasons to oppose the fur trade may include the negative effect the fur trade would have on the beaver population.

Link to ⌘ **Geography** Discuss with students which explorer's route was the most direct.

Then and Now — THEN AND NOW Montreal

What geographical feature made Montreal an important center for trade and industry? It was located on the St. Lawrence River.
Main Idea and Details

 READING STRATEGY
Sequence

In the Lesson Review, students complete a Sequence graphic organizer. You may want to provide students with a copy of Transparency 12 to complete as they read the lesson. This graphic organizer can be seen on p. 21 of the PE.

ESL EXTEND LANGUAGE
ESL Support

Discuss Natural Resources Students identify different natural resources.

Beginning Make a list on the board of natural resources from the lesson, such as *fish, furs, timber,* and *soil.* Work with students to make picture dictionary entries for each term.

Intermediate Write on the board a list of natural resources from the lesson. Have students make a two-column chart. Ask them to list in the left column the resource that was traded and in the right column, its use; for example, *furs* and *beaver felt hats.* Students may add labeled drawings to each column if time permits.

Advanced Have students list the natural resources discussed in this lesson. Then have them describe each one and write a sentence explaining why it was important. You might want to have them keep a running list of natural resources as they continue on to other units.

 CURRICULUM CONNECTION
Science

- Scurvy was a common disease among sailors. Have students use the Internet or other library resources to research the symptoms of scurvy and what dietary changes can prevent it.
- Explain that once people learned how to prevent scurvy, they changed their eating habits. Have students make a list of foods sailors could take with them to prevent scurvy on the long voyages across the Atlantic.

Write the Essay

Plan and Prewrite

Read aloud the sentence on PE p. 23 stating the topic for the document-based essay. Discuss the topic and share with students the rubric by which their essays will be scored (see TE p. 21). Have students review the documents and their answers to the related questions.

Pages 14–15, photo: Possible answer: They used the Inca foundation because it was strong. The Inca style is plain, while the Spanish part has arches and towers.

Page 15, graphs: Between 1570 and 1620, Peru's native population decreased from 1.3 million to 0.6 million. The difference is 0.7 million.

Page 16, map: Possible answer: Connections between explorers and people in Latin America brought changes to both Latin America and Europe. Horses were brought to Latin America, and potatoes were brought to Europe.

Pages 18–19, illustration: Possible answer: They seem welcoming.

Page 19, map: Cartier met the Iroquois and the Huron after meeting the Micmac.

Page 20, photo: Because the Métis adapted the weaving craft from the French culture, the Métis sash and French scarves used a similar method of weaving.

Discuss Before students begin planning their essays, you may wish to have a class discussion to stimulate students' thinking. Ask students to explain how each document relates information or ideas about relations between Europeans and native peoples in Latin America and Canada. Remind students that the unit provides the historical context for their responses.

Use a Graphic Organizer Remind students that a prewriting tool such as a graphic organizer will help them write a better essay. Model on the board a Main Idea and Details graphic organizer.

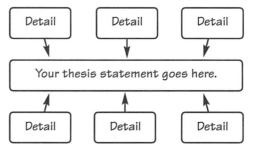

Tell students they may use other kinds of organizers as long as the organizers are suited to the topic. Once students complete their prewriting, have them write first drafts of their essays.

Content Tips Explain that the second bullet point on PE p. 23, "Write down in a few words the main idea you get from reading your answers," applies to each detail box on the graphic organizer. These ideas should support the thesis statement.

Evaluate and Revise

Check Content Once students have completed their first drafts, provide the following checklist to assist them in evaluating what they have written:

☐ Have I used information from the documents to draw my conclusion?

☐ Have I shown how information or ideas from each document are related to the topic?

☐ Have I included my own thoughts in the essay?

☐ Have I avoided simply summarizing the documents?

☐ Is my point clearly stated and explained?

☐ Is my essay logically organized?

☐ Do I use appropriate details to support my topic sentences?

☐ Have I avoided including statements that are unrelated to the topic?

Proofread After they have edited their essays for content, remind students to use a standard proofreading checklist to look for errors in spelling, grammar, and mechanics. Then have them write and submit the final drafts of their essays.

Score the Essay You may wish to use the rubric at right to score students' essays. If you have emphasized particular thinking or writing strategies during the study of Unit 2, you may wish to modify the rubric to include those skills.

Scoring Rubric
Unit 2 Document-Based Essay

4
- Shows superior understanding of the topic.
- Relates each document to the topic of early relations between Europeans and native peoples.
- Includes numerous insights (conclusions, inferences) that are well explained and supported by the documents.
- Includes no factual or mechanical errors.

3
- Shows reasonable understanding of the topic.
- Relates most of the details from the document to the topic of early relations between Europeans and native peoples.
- Includes some insights (conclusions, inferences) that are clear and for the most part supported by the documents.
- Includes very few factual or mechanical errors.

2
- Shows minimal understanding of the topic.
- Attempts to relate some details from the documents to the topic of early relations between Europeans and native peoples.
- Includes details, quotes, or paraphrasing, but no insights (conclusions, inferences) into the topic.
- Includes a number of factual or mechanical errors.

1
- Shows little or no understanding of the topic.
- Does not attempt to relate details from the documents to the topic of early relations between Europeans and native peoples.
- Includes only vague references, if any, to the content of the documents.
- Includes many factual or mechanical errors.

0
- Uses no accurate data, or response is totally unrelated to the topic.
- Is either illegible or incoherent, and no sense can be made of the response.
- Paper is blank.

Pupil Edition page 24

Vocabulary and People

Sample answers:

1. Huayna Capac was an emperor of the Inca.

2. The Line of Demarcation was an imaginary line running north and south in the Atlantic Ocean; Portugal and Spain agreed that Portugal would control the land east of the line and Spain would control the land west of it.

3. Jacques Cartier was a French explorer who traded with the Micmac and other native groups; he claimed Quebec for the king of France; he explored the St. Lawrence River and its valley; he used the name "Canada" for the land.

4. The voyageurs were French fur traders.

5. The Métis were the children of voyageurs and Native American women; they developed their own culture.

Facts and Main Ideas

Sample answers:

1. There was a market for sugar in Europe that would bring a high price.

2. Native Americans and Europeans exchanged beaver furs, metal goods, cloth, and beads.

3. **Main Idea** Smallpox and civil war had weakened the Inca.

4. **Main Idea** Europeans and Native Americans had a relationship based on trade.

5. **Critical Thinking:** *Hypothesize* Possible answers: Traders might have simply used the passage for shipping, trading mostly between Europe and Asia. Cities might have grown up along the passage, or traders might have bypassed potential Native American trade partners as they hurried to Asia.

Write About History

1. Students' journal entries should include details about Inca life and the Spanish attitude toward the Inca.

2. Students' travelogues should include details about the geography of the region and the encounters with Native Americans.

3. Students' letters might include details from the art on PE p. 19.

Read on Your Own

John Cabot, by Tanya Larkin (Powerkids Press, ISBN 0-823-95553-2, 2001) **Easy**

Lost Treasure of the Inca, by Peter Lourie (Boyds Mills Press, ISBN 1-563-97743-5, 1999) **Easy**

Beyond the Sea of Ice: The Voyages of Henry Hudson, by Joan Elizabeth Goodman (Mikaya Press, ISBN 0-965-04938-8, 1999) **On-Level**

The Incas, by Kathryn Hinds (Benchmark Books, ISBN 0-761-40270-5, 1998) **On-Level**

Jacques Cartier, Samuel De Champlain and the Explorers of Canada, by Tony Coulter (Chelsea House Publishing, ISBN 0-791-01298-0, 1993) **Challenge**

Out of Many Waters, by Jacqueline Dembar Greene (Walker & Company, ISBN 0-802-77401-6, 1993) **Challenge**

Colonial Life in the Americas

Unit Overview

The 1600s and 1700s were a period of colonial growth in North America for France and England. France established colonies in the area known as New France, and settlers there established communities based on agriculture and trade. Conflicts arose when England and France disagreed over boundaries. Struggles over the land ensued, including the nine-year French and Indian War. Spain's colonies in Latin America established an economy based on silver. Sugar, however, was the economic base for Portuguese Brazil. The growing demand for labor on the sugar plantations resulted in enslaved Africans being brought to Brazil and the Caribbean.

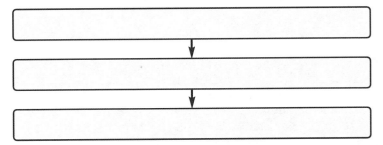

Draw a Sequence chart on the board and label it *Colonial Canada.* Ask students to recall the main events from Unit 2. Lead them to arrive at a one- or two-sentence summary of a main event, such as *The English and French claimed Canada and set up a system of trade with the Native Americans.* Record students' summaries in the first box. Explain to students that as they work through Unit 3, they should record main events in the order in which they happened. Repeat the procedure with a second Sequence chart labeled *Colonial Latin America.* At the end of the unit, have students share their completed charts in small groups.

SOCIAL STUDIES
Background

About the Slave Trade

- Merchants used the triangular trade route to carry trade items among the Americas, Europe, and Africa.
- The second leg of the triangular trade route, called the "Middle Passage," was the journey across the Atlantic to the Americas. Millions of Africans were shipped to the Americas from the 1400s through the 1800s. Almost 20 percent of enslaved Africans died while on slave ships.
- In 1888 Brazil banned slavery. The legacy of the slave trade remains, however. Brazil has nearly 1,000 *Quilombos,* or settlements founded by runaway slaves. Recently, residents of the Quilombos have demanded titles to these lands.

Pupil Edition page 25

SOCIAL STUDIES STRAND
Culture

- Explain that national and ethnic groups have played an important role in the history of Canada. National groups are groups of people who act on behalf of their country. For example, British soldiers who evicted Acadians from present-day Nova Scotia acted in the interest of Britain. Acadians, however, were an ethnic group—a group that shared a common background and culture.

- Relate that today Nova Scotia is home to varied ethnic groups who have contributed their customs and traditions to the culture of Canada. For example, there has been a Scottish presence in Nova Scotia for several centuries. After the Acadians left, Scottish immigrants settled in Nova Scotia (which means "New Scotland"). Today residents of Nova Scotia enjoy the Highland Games, an event that includes traditional Scottish dance, music, and sports. One sport, the "Ancient Stone Throw," is similar to the shot put. Competitors throw a stone that weighs more than 20 pounds.

Internet Links
To find out more about

- French settlements in Canada, visit **www.civilization.ca** key words *Acadians, New France*
- Sugar and slavery, visit **www.pbs.org** key words *slavery in Brazil, sugar plantations*
- Events in the United States at this time, visit **www.sfsocialstudies.com**

Colonial Canada

Pupil Edition pages 26–29

Objectives

- Identify how the government of New France differed from the government of the English colonies in its assumptions regarding power, authority, governance, and law.
- Describe the distribution of French settlers, the Iroquois, and the Huron in the early 1600s.
- Explain how James Wolfe led British forces to victory at Quebec.
- Explain how the Acadian ethnic group contributed to the cultures of Canada and the United States.

Vocabulary

seigneurs, p. 27

Quick Teaching Plan

If time is short, provide students with a map of North America. Have students work in pairs to mark key areas on the map as they read the lesson.

- Tell students to mark the areas occupied by the Huron and the Iroquois.
- Have students mark the area fought over in the French and Indian War and the location of the Battle of Quebec.
- Have students mark Acadia. Then have them mark the area in the United States to which many Acadians moved.

1 Introduce and Motivate

Preview To activate prior knowledge, ask students to suppose that a mayor offered free homes to families. In order to live in the house, however, each family would have to vote for the mayor in all the elections and follow all the mayor's rules. Have students brainstorm a list of pros and cons for participating in the program. Tell students that in Lesson 1 they will learn about the system of land ownership and the lives of settlers in Canada in the 1600s and 1700s.

2 Teach and Discuss

Quick Summary Many English and French settlers moved to North America in the 1600s and 1700s. Each group brought its own system of government. These differences and growing settlements led to boundary disputes. In addition, the Iroquois and the Huron were involved in boundary disputes.

Life in New France p. 27

- **Which group, the seigneurs or the tenant farmers, probably experienced greater economic growth in New France? Why?** The seigneurs probably experienced greater economic growth in New France because they received free land from the French king and collected rent from the tenant farmers. **Draw Conclusions**

✓ **REVIEW ANSWER** In New France, seigneurs owned land and rented it to tenant farmers. In many English colonies, settlers could own their own land. **Compare and Contrast**

A Time of Conflicts p. 27

- **How do you think the Iroquois attacks affected shipments of fur to Europe?** The attacks disrupted the trading system between the Huron and the French, so there were probably fewer furs going to Europe. **Draw Conclusions**

✓ **REVIEW ANSWER** New France's struggle with the Iroquois and its struggle with the English were both over land. **Compare and Contrast**

The French and Indian War p. 28

- **How might the Battle of Quebec have ended if James Wolfe had not found the Plains of Abraham?** Possible answers: The French might have been able to protect Quebec from British attack. It might have taken the British longer to win. **Hypothesize**

✓ **REVIEW ANSWER** The British gained control over the lands of New France east of the Mississippi. **Summarize**

The Acadians

pp. 28–29

- **Why do you think the Acadians did not take part in the conflicts between the French and the British?** Possible answer: The Acadians did not want to take sides because they wanted to live in peace and follow their own traditions. **Make Inferences**

✓ **REVIEW ANSWER** The Acadians' heritage was French, but they were under British control. When they refused to take sides and pledge their loyalty to Britain, the British worried that they would be loyal to France and forced them to move out of the colony. **Main Idea and Details**

3 Close and Assess

Summarize the Lesson Divide students into three groups. Have one group tell events from the lesson from the French point of view. Have the second group describe events from the English point of view. Have the third group describe events from the Iroquois point of view.

✓ Lesson 1 REVIEW

1. ⟳ **Compare and Contrast**

<table>
<tr>
<td>
• New France did not give settlers a voice in government.
• French colonists were subjects of their kings.
</td>
<td>
• The English colonies had elected assemblies that gave colonists a voice in government.
• English colonists were subjects of their kings.
</td>
</tr>
<tr>
<td align="center">**New France**</td>
<td align="center">**English Colonies**</td>
</tr>
</table>

2. Most French settlers lived to the east of Lake Ontario in the St. Lawrence Valley. Most Iroquois lived to the south of Lake Ontario. Most Huron lived to the north of Lake Ontario.

3. Wolfe found a path up the steep cliffs around Quebec City that led to the Plains of Abraham. The British fought the French on that field.

4. Elements of Acadians' culture include the Roman Catholic religion, ballads, fiddle music based on old French dances, and their own way of speaking.

5. Critical Thinking: *Express Ideas* Students might choose either colony, but they should cite differences in the governmental and land ownership systems in their answers.

Link to ⚬⚬ **Writing** You may wish to have students complete the assignment in small groups. Encourage them to include dialogue in their skits. Encourage groups to perform their skits for the class.

READING STRATEGY
Compare and Contrast

In the Lesson Review, students complete a graphic organizer like the one below. You may want to provide students with a copy of Transparency 14 to complete as they read the lesson.

Compare and Contrast

MEETING INDIVIDUAL NEEDS
Leveled Practice

Discuss Acadian Culture Have students describe various elements of Acadian culture.

Easy Have students work in small groups. Ask each group to identify the elements of Acadian culture that are presented in the lesson. **Reteach**

On-Level Have students discuss the role Acadian culture might have played in the lives of Acadians who moved to Louisiana. **Extend**

Challenge Have students use library resources to research more about Acadian culture. Ask students to share what they learn with the class. **Enrich**

SOCIAL STUDIES STRAND
Culture

Catholic Missionaries in Canada

- Early French settlers and missionaries brought Catholicism to Canada. They taught Christian beliefs and customs to the Huron.

- Later, the British restricted the religious freedom of Catholic French Canadians. However, in 1774 British Parliament passed the Quebec Act, which allowed religious freedom for French Canadians.

- Today, there are more than 12 million Catholics in Canada, making Catholics the largest religious group in that country. Catholics have contributed many customs and traditions to the culture of Canada, such as celebrations of Christmas and Easter.

LESSON 2

Pupil Edition pages 30–33

Objectives

- Identify the role that silver played in the Spanish colonial economy.
- Explain how sugar was important to the economy of Brazil.
- Explain how people of African ancestry contributed to the cultures of Brazil and the Caribbean.

Vocabulary

viceroy, p. 31; viceroyalty, p. 31; plaza, p. 31; peninsular, p. 31; Creole, p. 31

Quick Teaching Plan

If time is short, have students complete a Compare and Contrast graphic organizer with information about the groups of people discussed in the lesson.

- List the following groups on the board: viceroys, peninsulares, Creoles, mestizos, Native Americans, and people of African descent.
- Ask students to compare and contrast two of these groups using information from the lesson.

Colonial Latin America

1 Introduce and Motivate

Preview To activate prior knowledge, ask students to consider what they know about slavery in the United States. Ask them to name some kinds of work that enslaved people were forced to do. Then explain that in Lesson 2 they will learn how forced labor played an important role in the Spanish colonies and in Portuguese Brazil.

2 Teach and Discuss

Quick Summary Though the Spanish colonies flourished economically and culturally, there were divisions in society. Tensions among different groups led to rebellions by those who were oppressed. The economy of Portuguese Brazil was based on sugar. Much of the success of sugar plantations in Brazil and the Caribbean was due to the use of enslaved Africans. Over time, the cultures these Africans brought with them influenced the culture of the region.

Life in Spain's Colonies   p. 31

- **Why did the peninsulares and Creoles separate themselves from the rest of the people in Spain's colonies?** Possible answers: They may have felt superior to the mestizos and natives. Separating themselves may have helped them keep their culture and their position at the top of society. **Draw Conclusions**

✓ **REVIEW ANSWER** Because silver production became so important to the economy, Spain set up a government to make sure silver production ran smoothly. **Summarize**

Sugar and Slavery   p. 32

 SOCIAL STUDIES STRAND
Economics

Explain to students that productivity is determined by the relationship between the amount of goods produced and the amount of resources, such as land, labor, and capital, that is needed to produce the goods. The lower the cost of the resources, the higher the productivity—and the greater the profit.

- **How might life have been different for the plantation owners if they had not had slaves working for them?** Possible answer: Plantations would not have been as productive, so plantation owners would not have been as wealthy. If they had not been as wealthy, they would not have had so much power. **Hypothesize**

✓ **REVIEW ANSWER** Possible answers: There was much money to be made raising sugar cane. Sugar cane was exported to other countries. Also, sugar cane was grown using slave labor, which meant there was more profit for the plantation owners.
Draw Conclusions

An African Legacy   p. 33

- **What ethnic groups make up the majority of the population of many Caribbean islands?** Descendants of Africans make up the majority of the population. **Main Idea and Details**

✓ **REVIEW ANSWER** Many enslaved Africans adopted Christianity, but they incorporated their traditional style of singing and dancing into Catholic ceremonies and celebrations. **Summarize**

3 Close and Assess

Summarize the Lesson Divide students into three groups. Assign each group a section of the lesson. Have each group give a brief oral presentation about the events in that section and tell why those events were important.

✓ Lesson 2   REVIEW

1. **Summarize**
   [Box 1] The Spanish colonies grew rich from silver; many native people were forced to work in the silver mines.
   [Box 2] Peninsulares and Creoles were at the top of society; mestizos and native peoples were in the lowest positions of society.
   [Box 3] Sugar brought wealth to plantation owners in Brazil; enslaved Africans were forced to work on the plantations.

2. The silver mines kept many people working at mining, transporting, or providing supplies to Potosí and other mines.

3. The cities became the centers of government, economic activity, learning, and culture.

4. Enslaved Africans maintained some of their religious beliefs and practices and incorporated African singing and dancing styles into Catholic ceremonies; they brought a costumed celebration to Latin America that grew into Carnival.

5. **Critical Thinking: *Compare and Contrast*** Plantation workers suffered harsh conditions. Plantation owners grew wealthy and held power in Brazilian society.

Link to ∞ Economics Students might use the Internet or other library sources, but their paragraphs should contain accurate information. Have students cite their sources.

BIOGRAPHY
Sister Juana Inés de la Cruz

How might Sister Juana have influenced women in Mexico that came after her? Possible answer: She demonstrated that women could be writers and could take an interest in science and other learning. **Make Inferences**

Learn from Biographies She joined a convent where she could study on her own.

READING STRATEGY
Summarize

In the Lesson Review, students complete a Summarize graphic organizer. You may want to provide students with a copy of Transparency 6 to complete as they read the lesson. This graphic organizer can be seen on p. 33 of the PE.

ESL EXTEND LANGUAGE
ESL Support

Comparisons with Adjectives
Students will examine adjectives that end in -er and adjectives that end in -est.

Beginning Tell students that adjectives that end in -er compare two things, while adjectives that end in -est compare more than two things. Then make a two-column chart labeled *Compares Two Things* and *Compares More than Two Things*. Write the following words on the board: *richer, richest, older,* and *oldest.* Ask students to indicate the column in which each word belongs.

Intermediate Give students sentences that make comparisons, and have students provide the correct ending for each adjective. For example, "Alex is (rich) than Oscar. He is the (rich) of the five men."

Advanced Have students work with a partner to write a dialogue between two sugar plantation owners boasting about their plantations. Suggest that students use such words as *bigger, biggest, richer,* and *richest.*

CURRICULUM CONNECTION
Math

Calculate Difference in Years
Tell students that Harvard College (now Harvard University) was founded in 1636, but it was not the first university to be founded in the Americas.

- Have students use library resources to learn when the University of San Marcos in Peru and the National University of Mexico were founded. (1551)

- Have students calculate the difference in years between the founding of Harvard and the other two universities. (85 years)

Write the Essay

Plan and Prewrite

You may wish to have students use the documents in this unit to write an essay about the types of work performed in the economies of colonial Latin America and Canada. Discuss the topic and share with students the rubric that will be used to score their essays (see TE p. 29). Have students review the documents and the answers they recorded on their DBQ Record Sheets.

Page 27, map: People farmed on narrow strips of land so that all farms had access to the river.

Page 29, illustration: Acadians processed cod that was caught in the waters off the coast. The area was rich in fish, an important resource.

Page 30, illustration: Workers loaded materials on the backs of llamas.

Page 31, image: The plaza is busy and crowded. People are buying and selling things.

Page 32, map: Sugar cane from Brazil was shipped to Europe; textiles from Europe were shipped to Africa; slaves from Africa were shipped to Brazil.

Page 35, illustration:
- The scene is located in a sugar mill. People are processing sugar cane.
- People are working by hand or running machines. They are dressed poorly.
- These people were probably poor. Life was difficult in a sugar mill during this time period because the operation depended on a great deal of physical labor.
- The people worked very hard. Running a sugar mill required people to do many kinds of work.
- People are processing sugar cane. They are working by hand or running machines. Answers may also include the following: People are carrying things, working at a furnace, and using animals to move a cart.

Discuss Before students begin planning their essays, you may wish to have a class discussion to stimulate students' thinking. Ask students to identify the types of work shown in the documents. Remind students that the unit provides historical context for their responses.

Use a Graphic Organizer Remind students that a prewriting tool such as a graphic organizer will help them write a better essay. Model on the board a Main Idea and Details graphic organizer.

Suggest that students begin by writing descriptive details in the detail boxes. If necessary, provide one sample detail. Explain that after they list some details about the work people are doing, students should think about their main ideas. Explain that their main ideas should be supported by the details in the boxes. They should use the information in the main idea box to write the topic sentence of their paragraphs.

Content Tips Tell students to use higher-level thinking strategies as they write their essays. For example, students could draw conclusions based on the documents about the influence different types of work may have had on people's lives.

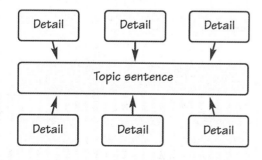

Evaluate and Revise

Check Content Once students have completed their first drafts, provide the following checklist to assist them in evaluating what they have written:

❑ Have I used information from the documents to draw my conclusion?

❑ Have I shown how information or ideas from each document are related to the topic?

❑ Have I included my own thoughts in the essay?

❑ Have I avoided simply summarizing the documents?

❑ Is my point clearly stated and explained?

❑ Is my essay logically organized?

❑ Do I use appropriate details to support my topic sentences?

❑ Have I avoided including statements that are unrelated to the topic?

Proofread After they have edited their essays for content, remind students to use a standard proofreading checklist to look for errors in spelling, grammar, and mechanics. Then have them write and submit the final drafts of their essays.

Score the Essay You may wish to use the rubric at right to score students' essays. If you have emphasized particular thinking or writing strategies during the study of Unit 3, you may wish to modify the rubric to include those skills.

Scoring Rubric
Unit 3 Document-Based Essay

4	• Shows superior understanding of the topic. • Relates each document to the topic of work. • Includes numerous insights (conclusions, inferences) that are well explained and supported by the documents. • Includes no factual or mechanical errors.
3	• Shows reasonable understanding of the topic. • Relates most of the details from the documents to the topic of work. • Includes some insights (conclusions, inferences) that are clear and for the most part supported by the documents. • Includes very few factual or mechanical errors.
2	• Shows minimal understanding of the topic. • Attempts to relate some details from the documents to the topic of work. • Includes details, quotes, or paraphrasing, but no insights (conclusions, inferences) into the topic. • Includes a number of factual or mechanical errors.
1	• Shows little or no understanding of the topic. • Does not attempt to relate details from the documents to the topic of work. • Includes only vague references, if any, to the content of the documents. • Includes many factual or mechanical errors.
0	• Uses no accurate data, or response is totally unrelated to the topic. • Is either illegible or incoherent, and no sense can be made of the response. • Paper is blank.

Pupil Edition page 36

Vocabulary, People, and Places

Sample answers:

1. The seigneurs were the landowners in the French system of land grants in New France.

2. Louis-Joseph de Montcalm was the general who led the French forces in the Battle of Quebec.

3. Acadia was an early French colony in eastern Canada, in what is now Nova Scotia.

4. Potosí was a city in the Andes Mountains where a rich silver mine was found.

5. A viceroy was a Spanish official who headed a region of the Spanish colonies.

Facts and Main Ideas

Sample answers:

1. Britain defeated France in the French and Indian War, and the French signed a treaty giving control of most of New France to Britain.

2. Silver and sugar were important goods produced in Latin America.

3. **Main Idea** French colonists struggled with the Iroquois and with English settlers in the 1600s and 1700s.

4. **Main Idea** In Spanish America, natives were forced to provide labor through a labor tax. In Portuguese Brazil, enslaved Africans worked on sugar plantations.

5. **Critical Thinking: *Predict*** Students might speculate that forced labor could lead to rebellion by the native peoples.

Write About History

1. Students' newscasts should include the importance that geography played in the battle.

2. Students' paragraphs should include details about how the landowners acquired the land and how they used labor.

3. Students' editorials should have a clearly stated opinion supported with facts from the text.

Read on Your Own

Evangeline for Children, by Alice Couvillon and Elizabeth Moore (Pelican Publishing Company, ISBN 1-565-54709-8, 2002) **Easy**

When the Viceroy Came, by Claudia Burr, Krystyna Libura, and Maria Cristina Urrutia (Groundwood Books, ISBN 0-888-99354-4, 1999) **Easy**

The African Slave Trade, by Shirlee P. Newman (Franklin Watts, Incorporated, ISBN 0-531-16537-X, 2000) **On-Level**

The Last of the Mohicans (Scribner Storybook Classics), by James Fenimore Cooper (Atheneum, ISBN 0-689-84068-3, 2002) **On-Level**

Evangeline and the Acadians, by Robert Tallant (Pelican Publishing Company, ISBN 1-565-54090-5, 2000) **Challenge**

Peru (Cultures of the World), by Kieran Falconer (Benchmark Books, ISBN 0-761-40179-2, 1996) **Challenge**

New Societies in Canada and Latin America

Unit Overview

The late 1700s were a time of discontent in colonies ruled by European powers. Just as the 13 American colonies began to fear Britain would impose more and more unfair laws and taxes, French Canadians started to fear that Britain would limit their freedoms. At the same time, people in Latin America resented what they saw as Spain's unreasonable taxes and its demands for unpaid labor. These tensions eventually led to fighting in all three parts of the Americas.

Pupil Edition page 37

Draw a K-W-L chart on the board and label it *1760–1780 in the Americas.* Ask students to tell you what they know about tensions between Europe and the Americas during the late 1700s. Record students' responses in the *K* column. Then ask them what questions they have about how these problems affected Canada and Latin America. Guide the discussion by asking students if they think there might have been events and conflicts similar to those that occurred in the 13 American colonies at that time. Record what students want to know in the *W* column of the chart. As students study the unit, record in the *L* column any answers they learn.

FYI SOCIAL STUDIES
Background

About Colonial Economics

Share the following information with students:

- European powers had a different perspective on taxes than the colonists and native peoples in the Americas had. People in Britain were taxed much more heavily than those in the North American colonies. When Britain's national debt nearly doubled during the French and Indian War, to Britain it seemed only fair that American colonists should contribute more revenue to Britain.

- Like other European nations, Spain had acquired colonies in order to become more wealthy and therefore more powerful. After investing time, money, and military force to establish American colonies, Spain felt justified in claiming a large share of the wealth produced by the mines, land, and labor of Latin America.

Additional Information

⚠ *To establish guidelines for your students' safe and responsible use of the Internet, use the Scott Foresman Internet Guide.*

Internet Links

To find out more about

- The rights of French settlers, visit **www.canadiana.org** key words *Quebec Act*

- Tupac Amaru II and the history of Peru, visit **www.pbs.org** key words *last Inca*

- Events in the United States at this time, visit **www.sfsocialstudies.com**

LESSON 1

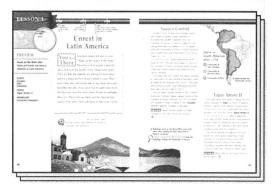

Pupil Edition pages 38–40

Objectives

- Explain how the economic system that Spain established in South America affected the native peoples there.
- Identify the role of Tupac Amaru II in the history of Latin America.
- Explain what abuses of power the participants in the Comunero Rebellion hoped to combat.

Vocabulary

Comunero Rebellion, p. 40

Quick Teaching Plan

If time is short, have students create a Venn diagram with the labels *Tupac Amaru's Rebellion* and *Comunero Rebellion.*

- As students read, have them take notes about each rebellion.
- After they read, have students complete the Venn diagram with information about when and where the rebellions took place, who was involved, and why they rebelled.

Unrest in Latin America

1 Introduce and Motivate

Preview To activate prior knowledge, ask students to tell about ways they have worked to earn money. Discuss how they would feel if they were forced to give up much of that money. Relate those feelings to how early colonists felt about high taxes. Tell students that as they read Lesson 1, they will learn how people in Latin America reacted to taxes paid to a foreign power.

2 Teach and Discuss

 Quick Summary When Spain began to demand higher taxes and more forced labor, colonists in many parts of Latin America rebelled.

Spain's Control p. 39

- **What did Spain demand of the people living in its Latin American colonies? Why do you think native people had gone along with Spanish demands for so many years?** Spain demanded more taxes. Possible answer: When life was not quite so hard, the cause was not worth dying for. As conditions got worse, people were willing to fight. **Draw Conclusions**

✓ **REVIEW ANSWER** The new line of kings that took over in Spain wanted to get more profits from the colonies.
🕤 **Cause and Effect**

Tupac Amaru II p. 39

- **Why do you think José Condorcanqui took the name Tupac Amaru II?** He wanted to show that he represented the native peoples, not the Spanish. **Draw Conclusions**

✓ **REVIEW ANSWER** It disrupted the colony's economy and showed natives that they could work together with the Creoles.
🕤 **Cause and Effect**

The Comunero Rebellion p. 40

- **What message did the Comunero rebels' slogan try to communicate to Spain?** The rebels did not want independence from Spain, but only to be treated fairly. **Draw Conclusions**

✓ **REVIEW ANSWER** Both rebellions were struggles between Spanish powers and native peoples, had support from mestizos and Creoles, and were protests against taxes. **Compare and Contrast**

3 Close and Assess

Summarize the Lesson Start an outline on the board. Use the lesson subheads for Roman numerals I, II, and III. Have students suggest the most important points to include under each.

✓ Lesson 1 REVIEW

1. 🕐 **Cause and Effect**

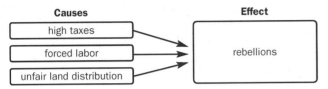

Causes	Effect
high taxes	
forced labor	rebellions
unfair land distribution	

2. Spain split Peru into two additional parts and appointed more Spanish-born officials in its colonies.

3. He led a revolt in Peru that spread to Bolivia and Argentina.

4. The Comunero Rebellion was a protest by native people in Colombia against Spain's high taxes, unfair land distribution, and labor abuses.

5. Critical Thinking: *Evaluate* Possible answer: No, because most of the work was done by the natives, but most of the wealth went to Spain.

Link to 〜 Geography Students' reports should show that they can successfully use an atlas along with other reference materials. Reports should include information on at least one important landform, waterway, and city in each country.

FACT FILE

Revolt Against Spain

Have students use the map key to interpret the events shown on the map. Help them connect the information on the line graph to what was happening in Peru during this time period.

- **What do you think might have caused the trend shown on the line graph?** As conditions grew worse for people, they might have been more likely to rebel. **Draw Conclusions**
- **Using information from the map and the graph, write a statement about what was happening in Latin America during the 1700s.** Possible answer: Native peoples in Latin America were growing more unhappy with what they saw as unfair treatment by Spain, and they rebelled. **Summarize**

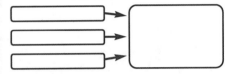

READING STRATEGY
Cause and Effect

In the Lesson Review, students complete a graphic organizer like the one below. You might want to provide students with a copy of Transparency 23 to complete as they read the lesson.

Cause and Effect

MEETING INDIVIDUAL NEEDS
Leveled Practice

Make a Presentation Remind students that Tupac Amaru II used peaceful means before leading a rebellion. Ask students to give reasons why Peruvians were unhappy.

Easy Ask students to make a poster with a map showing the countries that Tupac Amaru II led in the rebellion and a list of the causes of the uprising. Invite students to give a presentation about their poster. **Reteach**

On-Level Ask partners to write and give a speech the Inca leader might have made to persuade Spanish authorities to treat native workers more fairly. **Extend**

Challenge Ask students to research the events of Tupac Amaru II's life and the rebellion he led. Have them present their findings in a dramatic presentation with narration. **Enrich**

CURRICULUM CONNECTION
Art

Study Inca Art

- Provide books showing Inca art. Have students find and discuss patterns and symbols in the artwork.
- Have students draw, paint, or make from clay their own artwork inspired by Inca designs. Provide time for students to show and explain their work.

LESSON 2

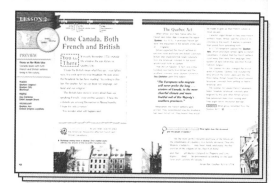

Pupil Edition pages 42–46

Objectives

- Explain how the Quebec Act offered basic civil values such as justice and equality to French Canadians.
- Explain how French Canadians and American colonists viewed the American Revolution differently.
- Describe how French fur traders in the 1700s affected westward migration in the 1800s.

Vocabulary

Quebec Act, p. 43; United Empire Loyalists, p. 44

Quick Teaching Plan

If time is short, have students prepare an outline of the lesson.

- As they read the lesson independently, have them write down the main idea of each section.
- For each main idea, have students list supporting details found in the section.

One Canada, Both French and British

1 Introduce and Motivate

Preview To activate prior knowledge, ask students to describe a time they felt they were treated unfairly. Have them tell why people in the 13 colonies might have had similar feelings. Explain that in Lesson 2 they will learn why some Canadian colonists feared they might be treated unfairly and how Britain responded.

2 Teach and Discuss

Quick Summary Great Britain passed the Quebec Act to calm the fears of French Canadians. This added to tensions in the American colonies. French Canadians chose not to support the colonists in their revolution, and American troops attempted but failed to take over key Canadian cities. Meanwhile, voyageurs pushed westward, setting the stage for Canadian expansion.

The Quebec Act   p. 43

- **According to Guy Carleton, why did many Europeans prefer to move to the southern colonies instead of to Quebec?** They preferred the warmer climate and more productive land to Canada's long winters. **Main Idea and Details**

✓ **REVIEW ANSWER** French Canadian settlers benefited because they were allowed to keep their culture and laws.
🕃 **Cause and Effect**

War Comes to Canada   p. 44

- **Suppose that the French Canadians did support the Americans in their revolution. How might North America be different today?** Students might speculate on Canadian territory being part of the United States or on French influences on American culture and society. **Make Inferences**

✓ **REVIEW ANSWER** American forces were unable to take Quebec City and were pushed back by the arrival of 10,000 British reinforcements. 🕃 **Cause and Effect**

The Move to Canada   pp. 44–45

- **Describe the Loyalists who settled in Quebec.** Most were farmers looking for fertile land to farm. Some 2,000 were Native Americans who had sided with the British. **Summarize**

MAP SKILL Answer About 200 miles

✓ **REVIEW ANSWER** Some were loyal to the king of Britain, some joined family members in Canada, some believed the 13 colonies would fail, and some were promised freedom from slavery.
🕃 **Cause and Effect**

SOCIAL STUDIES STRAND
Economics

Making a New Life in Nova Scotia

When thousands of Loyalists poured into Nova Scotia, the government gave them free land. Free land was not enough to ensure that Loyalist immigrants would be able to make a living. Those who had lived in cities were often unskilled at farming. Although some managed to make a living, others were unable to overcome the challenges of a harsh climate and poor farmland and returned to the 13 colonies.

Beyond European Settlements p. 46

• **How did the voyageurs' way of making a living affect the expansion of Canadian settlement?** Trading with trappers required them to travel to new lands that were later settled by other Canadians. ⊙ **Cause and Effect**

✓ **REVIEW ANSWER** The voyageurs moved west so they could trade with western trappers. ⊙ **Cause and Effect**

3 Close and Assess

Summarize the Lesson Read each lesson subhead aloud and ask a volunteer to summarize the section in a few sentences.

✓ Lesson 2 REVIEW

1. ⊙ **Cause and Effect**
   Cause: Carleton urges Britain to ease French settlers' fears.
   Cause: American colonists fear an invasion of British forces from Canada.
   Effect: Nova Scotia grows so much that it is divided to create New Brunswick.

2. The Quebec Act brought equality to French Canadians by allowing them to keep their own customs rather than having to adopt British customs.

3. French settlers felt the disagreement was between the American colonies and Britain and that it didn't have anything to do with French colonists in Canada.

4. Some United Empire Loyalists brought to Canada their ideas about loyalty to the king of England. Many Loyalists had been townspeople and merchants and brought with them the skills to become government and business leaders. Others had been frontier farmers and were willing to work under difficult circumstances to start new farms.

5. **Critical Thinking:** *Express Ideas* Possible answer: If the voyageurs had not challenged the Hudson Bay Company, settlement in the west may not have occurred until much later.

Link to ⌒⌒ Writing Students' letters should show an understanding of the rights and issues that were important to French Canadians.

READING STRATEGY
Cause and Effect

In the Lesson Review, students complete a graphic organizer like the one below. You might want to provide students with a copy of Transparency 20 to complete as they read the lesson.

Cause and Effect

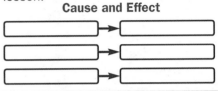

EXTEND LANGUAGE
ESL Support

Leaders and Colonists Explain to students that the text includes different words for groups of people who lived in the colonies and different words for some leaders there.

Beginning Explain to students the meaning of the word *leader.* Provide examples of leaders with whom they might be familiar at school or in their community. Then have students identify leaders from the lesson.

Intermediate Give simple explanations for the words *king, governor, chief, townspeople, merchants, farmers,* and *settlers.* Have students decide whether each word names a leader or a group of colonists.

Advanced Have students create a T-chart with the headings *Leaders* and *Groups of Colonists.* Ask them to find in the text words that fit in each category and record them.

Write the Essay

Plan and Prewrite

Have a volunteer read aloud the sentence on PE p. 47 stating the topic for the document-based essay. Discuss the topic and share with students the rubric by which their essays will be scored (see TE p. 37). Have students review the documents and their answers to the related questions.

Pages 38–39, image: Possible answer: In the photograph, you can see mountains in the background. The buildings have made the landscape less natural and from some places, you probably cannot even see the mountains because of the buildings.

Page 41, map: Mexico, Colombia, Peru, Bolivia, and Paraguay

Page 41, graph: The number of uprisings increased over time.

Page 43, quotation: It gives the people of Quebec the right to practice their own religion and the right to keep their own civil and property laws.

Page 44, map: Montgomery's troops, which affected both Montreal and Quebec City

Page 45, image: Possible answer: They had to travel in covered wagons over poor roads. If they faced some kind of emergency on the road, they had to wait for help to come by.

Discuss Before students begin planning their essays, you may wish to have a class discussion to stimulate students' thinking. Ask students what events are related to each document and what changes came about as a result of the events mentioned or portrayed in the documents. Remind students that the unit provides the historical context for their responses.

Events	Changes	Notes

Use a Graphic Organizer Remind students that a prewriting tool such as a graphic organizer will help them write a better essay. Model on the board a three-column chart similar to the one shown at left.

Suggest that students list in the first column the events they will discuss in their essays. In the second column, students should list the changes that resulted from each event. Point out that the third column is for students' own thoughts about each document and its relationship to the topic or to other documents.

Tell students they may use other kinds of organizers, as long as the organizers are suited to the topic. Once students complete their prewriting, have them write first drafts of their essays.

Content Tips Remind students that their essays should not simply describe, quote, or paraphrase the documents. It is important that students use what they learn from the documents to explain how the documents are related to events that caused change. Encourage students to use higher-level thinking strategies as they study the documents. If necessary, review strategies such as analyzing, evaluating, making inferences, and drawing conclusions.

Evaluate and Revise

Check Content Once students have completed their first drafts, provide the following checklist to assist them in evaluating what they have written:

☐ Have I used information from the documents to draw my conclusion?

☐ Have I shown how information or ideas from each document are related to the topic?

☐ Have I included my own thoughts in the essay?

☐ Have I avoided simply summarizing the documents?

☐ Is my point clearly stated and explained?

☐ Is my essay logically organized?

☐ Do I use appropriate details to support my topic sentences?

☐ Have I avoided including statements that are unrelated to the topic?

Proofread After they have edited their essays for content, remind students to use a standard proofreading checklist to look for errors in spelling, grammar, and mechanics. Then have them write and submit the final drafts of their essays.

Score the Essay You may wish to use the rubric at right to score students' essays. If you have emphasized particular thinking or writing strategies during the study of Unit 4, you may wish to modify the rubric to include those skills.

Scoring Rubric
Unit 4 Document-Based Essay

4	• Shows superior understanding of the topic. • Relates each document to change in Latin America and Canada. • Includes numerous insights (conclusions, inferences, analysis, evaluations) that are well explained and supported by the documents. • Includes no factual or mechanical errors.
3	• Shows reasonable understanding of the topic. • Relates most of the documents to change in Latin America and Canada. • Includes some insights (conclusions, inferences, analysis, evaluations) that are clear and for the most part supported by the documents. • Includes very few factual or mechanical errors.
2	• Shows minimal understanding of the topic. • Attempts to relate some documents to change in Latin America and Canada. • Includes description, quotes, or paraphrasing, but no insights (conclusions, inferences, analysis, evaluations) into the topic. • Includes a number of factual or mechanical errors.
1	• Shows little or no understanding of the topic. • Does not attempt to relate documents to change in Latin America and Canada. • Includes only vague references, if any, to content of the documents. • Includes many factual or mechanical errors.
0	• Uses no accurate data, or response is totally unrelated to the topic. • Is either illegible or incoherent, and no sense can be made of the response. • Paper is blank.

Pupil Edition page 48

Vocabulary and People

Sample answers:

1. Tupac Amaru II was a wealthy mestizo who led a revolt against Spanish power in Peru, Bolivia, and Argentina.

2. The Comunero Rebellion was a struggle between Spanish powers and native peoples, had support from mestizos and Creoles, and was a protest against taxes.

3. The Quebec Act was a British law that protected the rights of French colonists to keep their language, laws, religion, and land.

4. Guy Carleton was the governor of Quebec who urged Britain to take actions to ease the fears of French colonists so they would not rebel.

5. United Empire Loyalists were settlers who moved from the 13 colonies to Canada because they did not want to take part in the revolt against Britain.

Facts and Main Ideas

Sample answers:

1. Spain wanted to tighten control over Latin America in order to increase the wealth it got from its colonies.

2. American colonists feared an invasion of British forces from Canada.

3. **Main Idea** Latin American rebellions were a response to Spain's high taxes, its abuse of laborers, and its unfair land distribution.

4. **Main Idea** The American Revolution made the British pass the Quebec Act to try to avoid similar problems in Canada. It caused Loyalists to immigrate to Canada, which changed the nature of Nova Scotia. It also led to battles on Canadian soil.

5. **Critical Thinking:** *Compare and Contrast* Like French settlers, the Indians of Latin America were being governed by a foreign power with a different language and culture. Both had to pay taxes to those who governed them and both feared losing their land. The Latin American Indians were also put into forced labor by their rulers, but the French Canadians were not.

Write About History

1. Students' compositions should be in the form of diary entries. The two entries should include factual details about events during and after the attack on Quebec as well as reactions and feelings they think a young French Canadian would have.

2. Students' letters might mention geographical features and towns along the way as well as historical events that took place during that time. The letters should also give reasons for the family's move.

3. Students' editorials should give two or more opinions about how the Spanish should change their treatment of native peoples. Students should include persuasive arguments to support each opinion.

Read on Your Own

Peru, by Elaine Landau (Children's Press, ISBN 0-516-27019-2, 2000) **Easy**

Welcome to Colombia, by Bee Hong Lim and Leslie Jermyn (Gareth Stevens, ISBN 0-8368-2508-X, 2000) **Easy**

The Grandchildren of the Incas, by Matti A. Pitkanen with Ritva Lehtinen and Kari E. Nurmi (Carolrhoda Books, ISBN 0-87614-397-4, 1991) **On-Level**

The Iroquois: The Six Nations Confederacy, by Mary Englar (Bridgestone Books, ISBN 0-736-81353-5, 2002) **On-Level**

Colombia, by Marion Morrison (Children's Press, ISBN 0-516-21106-4, 1999) **Challenge**

The Fur Traders, by Robert Livesey (Stoddart Kids, ISBN 0-7737-5304-4, 1989) **Challenge**

Creating Colonies and New Nations

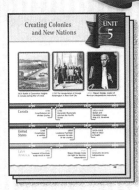

Pupil Edition page 49

Unit Overview

The late 1700s and early 1800s were a time of change in Canada and Latin America. Canada acquired new lands, sent explorers to investigate them, and established laws to meet the needs of a diverse population. At the same time, the ideas that inspired independence in the United States and in France also led Latin Americans to seek freedom and equality.

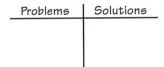

Problems	Solutions

Draw a two-column chart on the board and label the columns *Problems* and *Solutions*. Ask students to recall reasons why American colonists sought independence from Britain. List their responses in the *Problems* column on the chart. Then ask students how the problems were solved. List these responses in the *Solutions* column. As students study this unit, have them list problems with governments in Canada and Latin America and the ways these problems were solved. Then have them describe the similarities and differences among situations in the United States, Canada, and Latin America.

SOCIAL STUDIES
Background

Share the following information with students:

Canadian Government

• Concepts of government can be used to answer questions about how people should live their lives together. Through the Constitutional Act of 1791, the British government helped French and English Canadians live in peace by providing governments based on each group's traditions. Although both provinces followed the English Criminal Code, Lower Canada continued to follow French civil law. Canada still benefits from one change brought about by the Constitutional Act of 1791: the people elect their lawmakers.

Economic Decisions in Latin American Independence

• Nations must make economic decisions about the production and distribution of goods and services. Conflicts over who should make these decisions contributed to the fight for independence in Latin America. After Venezuela gained its independence from Spain, it also gained the right to choose its own trade partners. The newly independent country began to export coffee, a crop that proved to be very profitable. Coffee production dominated the economy of Venezuela into the 1900s, when petroleum became the country's leading export.

Additional Information

⚠ *To establish guidelines for your students' safe and responsible use of the Internet, use the Scott Foresman Internet Guide.*

Internet Links

To find out more about

• Explorers in Canada, visit **www.pbs.org**
key words *Alexander Mackenzie, North West Company*

• Independence in Haiti, visit **www.pbs.org**
key words *Toussaint L'Ouverture, Saint Domingue*

• Events in the United States at this time, visit **www.sfsocialstudies.com**

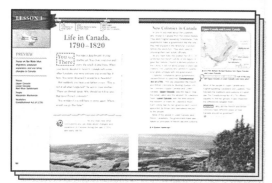

LESSON 1

Pupil Edition pages 50–53

Objectives
- Discuss how the migration of Loyalists influenced the beliefs, ideas, and laws of Canada.
- Explain how the need for natural resources led to exploration of western Canada in the late 1700s and early 1800s.
- Describe how people in Canada and the United States viewed the War of 1812 from different perspectives.

Vocabulary
Constitutional Act of 1791, p. 51

Quick Teaching Plan

If time is short, have students copy the following list of groups of people in Canada: Loyalists, French Canadians, British colonists.

- As students read the lesson independently, have them identify ways these groups shared customs, traditions, beliefs, ideas, or languages.

Life in Canada, 1790–1820

1 Introduce and Motivate

Preview To activate prior knowledge, ask students to name rules the school has established about how students should get along together. Tell students they will learn how the government in Canada passed a law that was designed to help people live in peace.

 You Are There The Loyalists who left the United States and settled in Quebec found themselves in a wilderness. In addition to the new landscape, they now had to follow unfamiliar French laws. Have students describe how Loyalists might have felt as they began life in a new land.

2 Teach and Discuss

Quick Summary Britain responded to disagreements between French-speaking and English-speaking Canadians by passing a law that offered equality for the two groups while respecting their differences. Canada expanded westward during the late 1700s and early 1800s. Explorers paved the way for traders and settlers. In the War of 1812, British and Canadian forces successfully defended Canada against American invasion. As a result of the war, Canadians gained a greater sense of unity.

New Colonies in Canada   p. 51

- **How do you think the Constitutional Act of 1791 showed that the government could answer questions about how people should live their lives together?** It showed that the government could satisfy the needs of both French-speaking and English-speaking Canadians by allowing the colonies to have governments based on each group's traditions and customs. **Make Inferences**

✓ **REVIEW ANSWER** The two groups followed different traditions, laws, and customs, and they were used to different forms of government. ⊙ **Draw Conclusions**

Exploring Western Canada   p. 52

- **Why do you think the North West Company wanted to find more natural resources?** If the company had more natural resources, it would have more things to trade. **Make Inferences**

✓ **REVIEW ANSWER** They might have established trading posts and settlements. They probably cleared the land for farming.
⊙ **Draw Conclusions**

Canada and the War of 1812 pp. 52–53

- **There were claims that the British were supplying weapons to Native Americans in the Ohio Valley. How might those claims have helped lead to war between Britain and the United States?** Settlers might have been afraid that they would be attacked by the Native Americans. ⊙ **Draw Conclusions**

✓ **REVIEW ANSWER** Although neither side won the war, both sides claimed victory. **Main Idea and Details**

3 Close and Assess

Summarize the Lesson Tell students to examine the vertical time line on p. 53. Ask them to summarize the lesson by explaining the significance of each event on the time line.

✓ Lesson 1 REVIEW

1. ⊙ **Draw Conclusions**

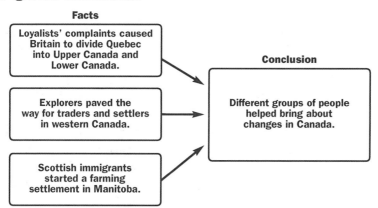

Facts

Loyalists' complaints caused Britain to divide Quebec into Upper Canada and Lower Canada.

Explorers paved the way for traders and settlers in western Canada.

Scottish immigrants started a farming settlement in Manitoba.

Conclusion

Different groups of people helped bring about changes in Canada.

2. Loyalists resented laws that favored French-speaking Canadians. They expected to have a government that allowed them to choose their own officials.

3. The Act split Quebec into two colonies. The government of Upper Canada followed the traditions of English law. The government of Lower Canada was based on French law and customs.

4. Explorers sent by the company discovered important waterways in western Canada. Traders and settlers migrated to western Canada.

5. **Critical Thinking: *Cause and Effect*** Possible answer: Canadians felt proud of themselves for having won. People in the United States might have felt Canadians should not feel so proud because they did not feel the Canadians actually won.

Link to ⚭ Geography Students should identify Ontario for Upper Canada and Quebec for Lower Canada.

READING STRATEGY
Draw Conclusions

In the Lesson Review, students complete a graphic organizer like the one below. You may want to provide students with a copy of Transparency 23 to complete as they read the lesson.

Draw Conclusions

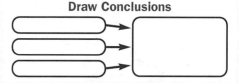

EXTEND LANGUAGE
ESL Support

Examine Words That Identify Groups of People Work with students to learn words that identify nationality.

Beginning Explain that words that identify nationality often end in *-an* or *-ian.* Point out *American* and *Canadian* on p. 52 and provide definitions. Model the words and have students repeat them after you.

Intermediate Start with the "Beginning" activity. Then explain that words that identify nationality also frequently end in the suffix *-ish.* Have students locate *British* on p. 52 and name the country from which this group of people comes.

Advanced Ask students to list all the words on p. 52 that identify nationality. Have students organize the words in a chart by word ending.

CURRICULUM CONNECTION
Literature

Learn More About the War of 1812 Have students read more about the War of 1812 and then prepare a report about this conflict.

Battles of the War of 1812, by Diane Smolinski (Heinemann Library, ISBN 1-403-40171-3, 2002) **Easy**

The War of 1812, by Rebecca Stefoff (Benchmark Books, ISBN 0-761-41060-0, 2000) **On-Level**

The Defenders, by Robert Livesey (Stoddart Kids, ISBN 0-773-75665-5, 1999) **Challenge**

LESSON 2

Pupil Edition pages 54–57

Objectives

- Explain how changing ideas about equality led to a revolution in the Caribbean in the late 1700s.
- Discuss how important historic figures in Mexico contributed to the fight for independence from Spain.
- Describe how ideas about what governments can and should do led to independence movements in other Latin American countries in the early 1800s.

Vocabulary

mulattos, p. 55

Quick Teaching Plan

If time is short, have students create an expanded time line of the events in Lesson 2.

- Begin a time line on the board, starting with *1791: Enslaved people in Saint Domingue revolt against their owners.*
- Have students read independently. Then call on volunteers to come to the board and add events in chronological order.

Life in Latin America, 1790–1820

1 Introduce and Motivate

Preview To activate prior knowledge, ask students to brainstorm words they associate with freedom. Tell students that they will learn how ideas about freedom affected nations in Latin America.

2 Teach and Discuss

Quick Summary The ideas of freedom and equality that inspired revolutions in the United States and France spread throughout Latin America in the late 1700s and early 1800s. Haiti won independence from France. Mexico, Venezuela, Argentina, and Chile won independence from Spain.

Revolution in the Caribbean   p. 55

- **Why do you think Napoleon wanted to restore slavery to Saint Domingue?** Possible answer: Napoleon wanted to keep Saint Domingue a wealthy colony. He knew many people were needed to work on the sugar plantations, and enslaved people could do the work. ⟲ **Draw Conclusions**

✓ **REVIEW ANSWER** Some European landowners lived in wealth and comfort. Many European settlers were middle-class shopkeepers, soldiers, and artisans. Mulattos did not have the same rights as Europeans. Enslaved people had few rights. **Main Idea and Details**

Unrest in Mexico   p. 56

- **Why did people stop supporting Iturbide?** Because once he was emperor, he tried to claim too much power. **Cause and Effect**

✓ **REVIEW ANSWER** Mestizos and native peoples had almost no voice in the government. They may have followed Hidalgo because they thought he could change the government. ⟲ **Draw Conclusions**

 SOCIAL STUDIES STRAND
Economics

- Tell students that every nation must make economic decisions about what goods and services to *produce,* how to produce goods and services, and how the goods and services will be *distributed*, or who will get the goods and services. Nations also make decisions about the *exchange* and *consumption* (use) of goods and services.
- In a **command economy,** the government makes economic decisions. For example, the Spanish government made economic decisions for its Latin American colonies.
- In a **market economy,** such as a free-enterprise system, individuals make economic decisions. The United States and Canada both have market economies.

Continuing the Fight for Independence

pp. 56–57

- **Why do you think Spanish forces stayed in Venezuela after the country declared independence?** Possible answer: Spain did not want to give up control of the country.
  🔵 **Draw Conclusions**

  ✓ **REVIEW ANSWER** Possible answer: The people of Buenos Aires now believed they were powerful enough to defeat Spain.
  🔵 **Draw Conclusions**

3 Close and Assess

Summarize the Lesson Write the three subheads from this lesson on the board. Ask students to write one main idea and one detail for each section.

✓ **Lesson 2** **REVIEW**

1. 🔵 **Draw Conclusions**

```
┌─────────────────────────────────────┐
│  The late 1700s and early 1800s were │
│  a time when ideas of freedom and    │
│       equality led many countries    │
│        in Latin America              │
│        to seek independence.         │
└─────────────────────────────────────┘
        ↗              ↑              ↖
┌──────────────┐ ┌──────────────┐ ┌──────────────┐
│ Enslaved     │ │ Mestizos and │ │ People in    │
│ people in    │ │ native       │ │ Venezuela    │
│ Haiti        │ │ peoples in   │ │ demanded     │
│ revolted     │ │ Mexico       │ │ freedom      │
│ against      │ │ revolted     │ │ from Spain.  │
│ their French │ │ against      │ │              │
│ owners.      │ │ Spanish rule.│ │              │
└──────────────┘ └──────────────┘ └──────────────┘
```

2. Miguel Hidalgo led mestizos and native peoples in the fight for freedom. José Morelos formed a congress that wrote a constitution for Mexico based on equality and protection of rights.

3. Peninsulares held all the important jobs in government and had the most power in Mexico.

4. Latin Americans had to send all their resources to Spain. They could not trade with other countries. They had to buy Spanish goods. They resented Spain's control over their economies. This helped lead to Latin Americans' fight for independence.

5. Critical Thinking: *Draw Conclusions* Ideas about inequality among different groups led to conflict and revolution in the United States and France. These ideas also inspired people in Latin America. Conflicts began as people in Latin America fought for independence.

Link to ⟨∞⟩ Writing Students' letters should list such ideas as lack of freedom, inequality among groups of people, or lack of control over economic decisions.

THEN AND NOW
Mexican Independence Day

How do Independence Day celebrations in Mexico today honor the nation's history? Possible answer: People reenact the events of September 16, 1810, to show the importance Mexican independence still has today. **Express Ideas**

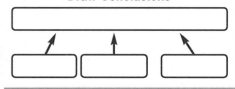

READING STRATEGY
Draw Conclusions

In the Lesson Review, students complete a graphic organizer like the one below. You may want to provide students with a copy of Transparency 1 to complete as they read the lesson.

Draw Conclusions

```
┌─────────────────────────────┐
│                             │
└─────────────────────────────┘
   ↑          ↑          ↑
┌──────┐  ┌──────┐  ┌──────┐
│      │  │      │  │      │
└──────┘  └──────┘  └──────┘
```

MEETING INDIVIDUAL NEEDS
Leveled Practice

Make a Presentation Tell students that citizenship includes an awareness of patriotic celebrations.

Easy Have students draw pictures to illustrate celebrations of Independence Day in Mexico. Discuss how these celebrations are similar to and different from July Fourth celebrations in the United States. **Reteach**

On-Level Have students find out about Independence Day in Haiti. Ask them to share their findings in an oral report. **Extend**

Challenge Ask students to use library resources to learn more about Toussaint L'Ouverture. Explain that even though Toussaint did not live to see independence in Haiti, his work helped bring independence to his country. Then have students compare Toussaint with Abraham Lincoln and Martin Luther King, Jr. Ask students to explain why people in Haiti or the United States might celebrate the lives of these people on national holidays. **Enrich**

Write the Essay

Plan and Prewrite

You may wish to have students use the documents in this unit to write an essay on different ideas about freedom in Canada and Latin America. Discuss the topic and share with students the rubric that will be used to score their essays (see TE p. 45). Have students review the documents and the answers they recorded on their DBQ record sheets.

Page 51, map: Lower Canada covered more area.

Page 52, photo: The image shows a wide river, a wide riverbank, and trees. This region might have attracted settlers seeking freedom because the land looks wide open and unsettled. Also, there were resources available for beginning a new life.

Pages 54–55, image: Plantation owners may have thought they needed enslaved workers because the plantations were very large and they needed many people to do the work.

Page 55, chart: Toussaint learned to read and write. He read books about individual rights before he was freed from slavery.

Page 56, photo: The broken chain is the symbol that represents a desire to be free. Possible answer: Yes, it is an effective symbol because it shows that the desire for freedom is strong enough to break through chains.

Page 59, letter excerpt:
- He means that slavery is not acceptable to people once they know what freedom is like.
- Ending slavery is the "most beautiful achievement"; it suggests that he thinks ending slavery is a noble and honorable thing.
- Toussaint would rather face death than return to slavery.
- He feels that ending slavery is worth any cost.

Discuss Before students begin planning their essays, you may wish to have a class discussion to stimulate students' thinking. Ask students to state how the various documents convey ideas about freedom. Remind students that the unit provides the historical context for their responses.

Use a Graphic Organizer Remind students that a prewriting tool such as a graphic organizer will help them write a better essay. Model on the board a Draw Conclusions graphic organizer.

Suggest that students complete the graphic organizer with details that tell the different ideas people in Canada and Latin America had about freedom. Tell students they may use other kinds of organizers, as long as the organizers are suited to the topic. Once students complete their prewriting, have them write first drafts of their essays.

Content Tips Tell students that they should not simply repeat the information from their graphic organizers in their essays. Explain that students should use the details as a starting point for their essays. Remind students that their essays should also state why ideas of freedom were important to people in the late 1700s and early 1800s.

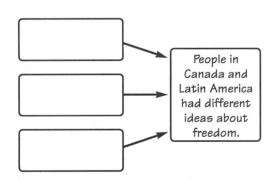

People in Canada and Latin America had different ideas about freedom.

Evaluate and Revise

Check Content Once students have completed their first drafts, provide the following checklist to assist them in evaluating what they have written:

- ❏ Have I used information from the documents to draw my conclusion?
- ❏ Have I shown how information or ideas from each document are related to the topic?
- ❏ Have I included my own thoughts in the essay?
- ❏ Have I avoided simply summarizing the documents?
- ❏ Is my point clearly stated and explained?
- ❏ Is my essay logically organized?
- ❏ Do I use appropriate details to support my topic sentences?
- ❏ Have I avoided including statements that are unrelated to the topic?

Proofread After they have edited their essays for content, remind students to use a standard proofreading checklist to look for errors in spelling, grammar, and mechanics. Then have them write and submit the final drafts of their essays.

Score the Essay You may wish to use the rubric at right to score students' essays. If you have emphasized particular thinking or writing strategies during the study of Unit 5, you may wish to modify the rubric to include those skills.

Scoring Rubric
Unit 5 Document-Based Essay

4	• Shows superior understanding of the topic. • Relates each document to the topic of freedom. • Includes numerous insights (conclusions, inferences) that are well explained and supported by the documents. • Includes no factual or mechanical errors.
3	• Shows reasonable understanding of the topic. • Relates most of the details from the documents to the topic of freedom. • Includes some insights (conclusions, inferences) that are clear and for the most part supported by the documents. • Includes very few factual or mechanical errors.
2	• Shows minimal understanding of the topic. • Attempts to relate some details from the documents to the topic of freedom. • Includes details, quotes, or paraphrasing, but no insights (conclusions, inferences) into the topic. • Includes a number of factual or mechanical errors.
1	• Shows little or no understanding of the topic. • Does not attempt to relate details from the documents to the topic of freedom. • Includes only vague references, if any, to content of the documents. • Includes many factual or mechanical errors.
0	• Uses no accurate data, or response is totally unrelated to the topic. • Is either illegible or incoherent, and no sense can be made of the response. • Paper is blank.

Pupil Edition page 60

Vocabulary and People

Sample answers:

1. The Constitutional Act of 1791 divided Quebec into Upper Canada and Lower Canada.

2. Explorer Alexander Mackenzie was the first European to cross Canada to the Pacific Ocean.

3. The Red River Settlement was a farming settlement established by Scottish immigrants in what is now Manitoba.

4. Mulattos were people of mixed African and European background who did not have the same rights as Europeans.

5. Toussaint L'Ouverture led a revolt to free enslaved people in Haiti.

6. Miguel Hidalgo was a Catholic priest who led the fight for Mexican independence.

Facts and Main Ideas

Sample answers:

1. Loyalists influenced this decision.

2. **Main Idea** The government of Upper Canada was based on traditions and customs of English law. The government of Lower Canada was based on principles of French law and customs.

3. Explorers traveled across Canada's western lands. They discovered major waterways.

4. When the people of France revolted against the king and landowners, this spirit of independence inspired enslaved people in Saint Domingue to revolt against their owners.

5. **Main Idea** Changing ideas about equality and resentment over Spain's economic policies were two reasons these countries fought for independence.

6. **Critical Thinking: *Compare and Contrast*** Similar: People in Mexico and the United States rebelled against European rule because they had no voice in government. Different: The nation against which people rebelled, the leadership in the colonies, and the length of time required to win independence differed.

Write About History

1. Students' poems might reflect ideas discussed in the unit. Students might also write about why freedom is important to them.

2. Students' newspaper stories should answer the following questions about Miguel Hidalgo: *Who was he? What did he do? When did he do it? Where did he do it? Why did he do it?* and *How did he do it?*

3. Students' editorials should reflect understanding of different points of view.

Read on Your Own

Laura Secord: A Story of Courage, by Janet Lunn (Tundra Books, ISBN 0-887-76538-6, 2001) **Easy**

Miguel Hidalgo Y Costilla: Father of Mexican Independence, by Frank De Varona (Millbrook Press Trade, ISBN 1-562-94863-6, 1995) **Easy**

Discovering Canadian Pioneers, by Marlene Gutsole and Reginald Gutsole (Oxford University Press, ISBN 0-195-41325-3, 1999) **On-Level**

Toussaint L'Ouverture, Lover of Liberty, by Laurence Santrey (Troll Associates, ISBN 0-816-72824-0, 1994) **On-Level**

The Loyal Refugees, by Robert Livesey (Stoddart Kids, ISBN 0-773-76043-1, 1999) **Challenge**

Mexico: 40 Activities to Experience Mexico Past and Present, by Susan Milord (Williamson Publishing, ISBN 1-885-59322-8, 1999) **Challenge**

Times of Change: 1822–1850

While groups in the United States were fighting against slavery and for women's rights, Latin American countries fought for independence from European control. With the exception of Brazil, which won its independence peacefully, these countries won their freedom through violent revolutions. The independent nations then began the task of establishing responsible governments. During the same time period, Canada experienced debates and rebellions over how it should be governed. These events led to unification of Upper Canada and Lower Canada and to the formation of responsible government that took steps toward political independence from Britain.

Pupil Edition page 61

Latin America	United States	Canada

Draw a Compare and Contrast chart on the board and label the squares *Latin America, United States,* and *Canada*. Ask students to fill in the center square with answers to the following questions: *From which country did the United States seek independence? How did it win independence? What happened as a result of independence?* As students study Unit 6, have them fill in similar information for Latin America and Canada.

SOCIAL STUDIES
Background

Share the following with students:

- Simón Bolívar is sometimes called the "George Washington of Latin America" because he was a great general who fought for independence. His birthday, like that of George Washington in the United States, is celebrated as a national holiday in some Latin American countries.

- Juana Azurduy de Padilla and her husband raised a small army to fight for Bolivian independence. When her husband was killed, Juana continued to fight. She eventually formed a small republic that held out, under siege, until Bolívar was able to join her forces.

Additional
Information

⚠️ *To establish guidelines for your students' safe and responsible use of the Internet, use the Scott Foresman Internet Guide.*

Internet Links

To find out more about

- Simón Bolívar, visit **www.historychannel.com** key words *Simón Bolívar*

- Canada's path to confederation, visit **www.histori.ca** key words *Durham Report*

- Events in the United States at this time, visit **www.sfsocialstudies.com**

SOCIAL STUDIES STRAND
Citizenship

- Explain to students that concepts such as civic life, politics, and government can be used to answer questions about what governments can and should do and about how citizens can support the proper use of authority.

- For example, in 1838, Juan Pablo Duarte started a movement with the goal of freeing the Dominican Republic from Haiti's rule. Many Dominicans supported this goal, and in 1844 Duarte helped the Dominican Republic achieve independence.

- In Canada, under the leadership of Reformers, citizens used tools such as lodging formal grievances, organizing marches, forming political coalitions, and voting to bring about changes in government.

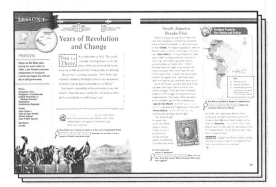

Pupil Edition pages 62–65

Objectives

- Explain how San Martín and Bolívar made significant contributions to the development of Latin America.
- Contrast the views of those who wanted to reform government in Mexico and those who opposed reform.
- Explain how Duarte made significant contributions to the development of Latin America.

Vocabulary

Cortés, p. 63

Quick Teaching Plan

If time is short, write the list of people from Lesson 1 on the board.

- As students read the lesson independently, have them write a sentence about the major accomplishment of each person.
- Have students use a map of Latin America to locate the country or countries associated with each person on the list.

Years of Revolution and Change

1 Introduce and Motivate

Preview To activate prior knowledge, ask students to explain why people in the United States celebrate Independence Day. Explain that in Lesson 1 they will learn why people in many Latin American countries had reason to celebrate in the early 1800s.

2 Teach and Discuss

Quick Summary Between 1822 and 1850, Latin America became free from European rule. Brazil gained freedom from Portugal without bloodshed. Most other Latin American countries gained freedom from Spain through revolutions. The independent nations then faced the challenge of setting up new governments.

South America Breaks Free p. 63

- **How do you think the history of some Latin American countries might be different if Simón Bolívar had not fought for independence?** Possible answer: Countries such as Colombia, Venezuela, Ecuador, and Peru might not have won independence from Spain until much later. **Make Inferences**

✓ **REVIEW ANSWER** Similar: Like other countries in South America, Brazil sought independence. Different: It claimed its independence without bloodshed. ☺ **Compare and Contrast**

**$ SOCIAL STUDIES STRAND
Economics**

Share the following information with students:

- This period saw the Industrial Revolution spread from Britain to the United States. Industrialization meant that goods could be produced more cheaply through improved productivity.
- The term *capital* refers to the machines, tools, and factories that can be used to produce goods. It also refers to money. Capital helps industrialization take root. For example, a large middle class means that more people can afford to buy the goods that are produced. Investors with capital help business owners build factories and buy equipment. Capital is also needed to build roads, railways, and so on, for getting goods to market quickly.
- Explain that conditions in Latin America during this time did not make it as likely a place for the Industrial Revolution to take hold. For example, there was not a large middle class to buy new types of goods. People needed their scarce capital to satisfy their basic needs and wants. There was also little capital to invest in factories and equipment.

Central America and Mexico p. 64

- **How did different views about what governments can and should do contribute to the United Provinces' breaking apart?** Possible answer: Different groups had different ideas about the purpose of government and what kind of government could best meet the needs of its people. Because the provinces disagreed about the best type of government, each province decided to choose its own government. **Express Ideas**

✓ **REVIEW ANSWER** They went from being ruled by Spain to governing themselves, but they also had civil wars.
ⓢ **Compare and Contrast**

Independence in the Dominican Republic p. 65

- **Why do you think people in the Dominican Republic rebelled against Haitian control?** Possible answer: The Dominican Republic had won independence from Spain. The people did not want to be controlled by another country. **Make Inferences**

✓ **REVIEW ANSWER** He organized the rebel force that won Dominican independence from Haiti. **Main Idea and Details**

3 Close and Assess

Summarize the Lesson Have students use the entries on the time line to summarize the lesson. Ask them to provide at least two details for each main idea.

✓ Lesson 1 REVIEW

1. ⓢ **Compare and Contrast**
   Before Independence: European control
   (Center of diagram) economic problems, political unrest
   After Independence: decisions about how to govern, civil war

2. Simón Bolívar was a Venezuelan general who led liberation forces in the north. José de San Martín was a general from Argentina who led the revolution in the south. Both won independence for their own and other countries.

3. Many groups united while they were trying to win freedom, but they divided and formed new alliances once they had won independence and had to decide on a system of government.

4. Duarte drove the Haitians out of the Dominican Republic.

5. **Critical Thinking:** *Make Inferences* Economic troubles and power struggles might have caused people to want change. People who held power after independence might have opposed change.

Link to — Art Encourage students to choose an event that affects a large number of people. Students' artwork should not only show the event but also reflect their thoughts or feelings about it.

READING STRATEGY
Compare and Contrast

In the Lesson Review, students complete a graphic organizer like the one below. You may want to provide students with a copy of Transparency 13 to complete as they read the lesson.

Compare and Contrast

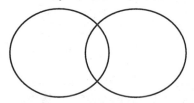

MEETING INDIVIDUAL NEEDS
Leveled Practice

Learn About Revolutionary Heroes Have students find out more about individuals who helped their nations win independence.

Easy Have students write tests in which the names of revolutionary heroes from Lesson 1 must be matched with clues about their accomplishments. Then have students exchange their tests with a partner. **Reteach**

On-Level Have students write a short speech that tells about the importance of one of the revolutionary heroes from Lesson 1. Then have others try to identify the hero. **Extend**

Challenge Have students research and report on Juana Azurduy de Padilla or another Latin American revolutionary hero from the 1800s. **Enrich**

Pupil Edition pages 66–69

Objectives

- Describe how the beliefs of French Canadians contributed to the different cultures of Canada during the mid-1800s.
- Explain the contributions of Mackenzie, Papineau, Durham, Baldwin, and LaFontaine to the development of Canada.
- Contrast the assumptions of Tories and Reformers regarding power, authority, governance, and laws.

Vocabulary

Ninety-two Resolutions of Grievances, p. 67; Durham Report, p. 68; responsible government, p. 68; Act of Union, p. 68

Quick Teaching Plan

If time is short, write the vocabulary terms on the board.

- As students read the lesson independently, have them write their own definition for each vocabulary term.
- Have students briefly explain how each term is related to changes in Canada between 1822 and 1850.

Canada Demands Change

1 Introduce and Motivate

Preview To activate prior knowledge, ask students to recall a time when people in the United States set aside their differences and worked together to bring about change. Tell students that in Lesson 2 they will learn how Canadians with differing viewpoints worked together to achieve responsible government.

2 Teach and Discuss

Quick Summary Tories and Reformers in Canada disagreed about who should control the government. These disagreements led to rebellions. Parliament united Upper Canada and Lower Canada, but it gave French Canadians less power, reduced representation, and left them with fewer protections than they had enjoyed. Finally, Reformers were elected to lead the Assembly. They helped unite Canadians to work toward the goal of responsible government and political independence from Britain.

The Rebellions of 1837   p. 67

- **What problem did the Reformers want to fix?** Citizens were not all given equal rights or equal treatment. **Main Idea and Details**

✓ **REVIEW ANSWER** Papineau wrote a formal complaint called the Ninety-two Resolutions of Grievances, which listed reforms needed to establish proper use of authority. **Summarize**

Working Toward Resolution   p. 68

- **Suppose you are a member of the British Parliament and have just received the Durham Report. Would you accept Lord Durham's recommendation of responsible government in Canada? Explain.** Students may accept or reject Durham's recommendation, but they should support their decisions logically. **Make Decisions**

✓ **REVIEW ANSWER** Parliament united Upper Canada and Lower Canada, but it did not adopt Durham's plan for responsible government. ☉ **Compare and Contrast**

Steps Toward Self-Government   pp. 68–69

- **Explain how Reformers used politics to support the proper use of authority.** Reformers united French-speaking and English-speaking people to vote for legislators who supported reform. **Analyze Information**

✓ **REVIEW ANSWER** Canadians elected Reformers, such as Baldwin and LaFontaine, to lead the Assembly. Because they were able to unite voters, the Reform Party took control of the legislature and brought responsible government to Canada. **Summarize**

3 Close and Assess

Summarize the Lesson Have volunteers play the parts of the people listed in the lesson preview. Each person should summarize how his accomplishment brought changes to Canada.

✓ Lesson 2 REVIEW

1. ☉ Compare and Contrast

Tories	Reformers
• Wanted Canada to be under the control of Britain and wealthy Tory groups • Did not want to change	• Wanted a constitution that would protect the rights of the majority • Wanted citizens to be given equal treatment

2. Britain's poor economy led British citizens to demand free trade. Parliament ended some trade restrictions and allowed Canada to trade in new markets.

3. Durham was a governor in British North America. He wrote a report that recommended responsible government and the unification of Upper Canada and Lower Canada.

4. The plan lessened their power to protect their culture and traditions.

5. Critical Thinking: *Make Generalizations* Possible answer: They might learn that it is possible for political leaders to work together to create positive change, even though they represent voters with different interests.

Link to ∽∞ Writing Students' letters should reflect understanding of the opposing views of Tories and Reformers and present logical reasons for supporting the Reformers.

FACT FILE

• **Tell how concepts of scarcity and resources help explain the state of the economy of Canada in 1837.** Land was the most important resource for Canadian farmers. Overuse of the land, followed by flooding, resulted in scarcity of crops and money earned from crops. Lack of resources and scarcity of capital resulted in economic problems. **Summarize**

READING STRATEGY
Compare and Contrast

In the Lesson Review, students complete a graphic organizer like the one below. You may want to provide students with a copy of Transparency 14 to complete as they read the lesson.

Compare and Contrast

EXTEND LANGUAGE
ESL Support

Examine Word Meaning Work with students to explore the meaning of *majority*.

Beginning Display two different colored sheets of paper. Ask students to vote on which color they like better. Record votes on the board. Introduce the word *majority* to describe the results.

Intermediate Point out that inside the word *majority* is the smaller word *major*. Ask students when they have heard the word *major*, such as in *major league*. When they understand that *major* means "big" or "important," help them arrive at a definition for *majority*.

Advanced Have students give examples of situations that are decided by majority vote. Then discuss reasons why majority rule is one of the values expressed in constitutions and laws.

CURRICULUM CONNECTION
Art

Design a Stamp

• Have students look again at the postage stamp honoring Simón Bolívar on PE p. 63. If possible, provide students with other examples of commemorative stamps.

• Have each student choose a person or event from Lesson 2 and design a commemorative stamp. Ask students to write a brief explanation about what their stamps depict.

Write the Essay

Plan and Prewrite

Read the sentence on PE p. 71 that gives the topic for the document-based essay. Discuss the topic and share with students the rubric by which their essays will be scored (see TE p. 53). Have students review the documents and their answers to the related questions.

Page 62, illustration: They seem to be greeting the new government with eagerness and excitement.

Page 63, stamp: The stamp honors Simón Bolívar. This suggests that Latin Americans value his contributions to their independence.

Page 63, map: Possible answer: Argentina and Chile were freed by San Martín.

Page 64, chart: One group favored a republic that would reduce the power of the church and encourage free trade. The other group favored a monarchy that would keep the church's privileged position and allow Spain to dominate trade.

Page 67, illustration: A well-equipped, formal army is firing on an ill-prepared rebel force. Consequences of the rebellion that are visible in the picture include the village burning in the background and rebels being wounded and fleeing.

Page 68, quote: Lord Durham's report recommended establishing responsible government and uniting Upper Canada and Lower Canada. Supporters of the report might have believed that it would end conflicts by helping French Canadians blend into English culture. Opponents may have feared that it would give French Canadians too much power, or they may have feared loss of French culture.

Discuss Before students begin planning their essays, you may wish to have a class discussion to stimulate students' thinking. Ask students to state how the various documents convey ways different groups in Canada and in Latin American countries expressed competing ideas about how to govern. Remind students that the unit provides the historical context for their responses.

Use a Graphic Organizer Remind students that a prewriting tool such as a graphic organizer will help them write a better essay. Have students create Venn diagrams to compare and contrast different ideas about how to govern in Canada and in Latin America.

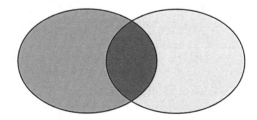

Tell students they may use other kinds of organizers, as long as the organizers are suited to the topic. Once students complete their prewriting, have them write first drafts of their essays.

Content Tips Reread the third bullet point on PE p. 71, "The paragraph should also support the topic sentence with ideas from your own knowledge and experience." Tell students to brainstorm what they know and think about how to govern. Explain that they may include these thoughts in their essays. Remind students that anything they include in their essays must support the topic sentences.

Evaluate and Revise

Check Content After students have completed their first drafts, provide the following checklist to assist them in evaluating what they have written.

❑ Have I used information from the documents to draw my conclusion?

❑ Have I shown how information or ideas from each document are related to the topic?

❑ Have I included my own thoughts in the essay?

❑ Have I avoided simply summarizing the documents?

❑ Is my point clearly stated and explained?

❑ Is my essay logically organized?

❑ Do I use appropriate details to support my topic sentences?

❑ Have I avoided including statements that are unrelated to the topic?

Proofread After they have edited their essays for content, remind students to use a standard proofreading checklist to look for errors in spelling, grammar, and mechanics. Then have them write and submit the final drafts of their essays.

Score the Essay You may wish to use the rubric at right to score students' essays. If you have emphasized particular thinking or writing strategies during the study of Unit 6, you may wish to modify the rubric to include those skills.

Scoring Rubric
Unit 6 Document-Based Essay

4	• Shows superior understanding of the topic. • Relates each document to the topic of competing ideas about how to govern. • Includes numerous insights (conclusions, inferences) that are well explained and supported by the documents. • Includes no factual or mechanical errors.
3	• Shows reasonable understanding of the topic. • Relates most of the details from the documents to the topic of competing ideas about how to govern. • Includes some insights (conclusions, inferences) that are clear and for the most part supported by the documents. • Includes very few factual or mechanical errors.
2	• Shows minimal understanding of the topic. • Attempts to relate some details from the documents to the topic of competing ideas about how to govern. • Includes details, quotes, or paraphrasing, but no insights (conclusions, inferences) into the topic. • Includes a number of factual or mechanical errors.
1	• Shows little or no understanding of the topic. • Does not attempt to relate details from the documents to the topic of competing ideas about how to govern. • Includes only vague references, if any, to content of the documents. • Includes many factual or mechanical errors.
0	• Uses no accurate data, or response is totally unrelated to the topic. • Is either illegible or incoherent. • Paper is blank.

Pupil Edition page 72

Vocabulary, People, and Places

Sample answers:

1. Dom Pedro I was the ruler of Brazil who declared independence from Portugal.

2. Simón Bolívar was a Venezuelan general who helped free Colombia, Venezuela, Ecuador, and Peru from Spanish rule.

3. Ayacucho, Peru, was the site of the last great victory that made South America free of Spanish rule.

4. Juan Pablo Duarte organized a rebel force that freed the Dominican Republic from Haitian rule.

5. The Act of Union united Upper Canada and Lower Canada, made English the official language of Canada, and reduced French representation in the legislature.

6. The United Province of Canada was the name given to the land made up of Canada East and Canada West, which had been Upper Canada and Lower Canada.

7. Robert Baldwin was a Reformer who helped bring responsible government to Canada in the 1840s.

8. Louis LaFontaine was a Reformer who worked with Baldwin to unite Canadians and bring responsible government to Canada.

Facts and Main Ideas

Sample answers:

1. Political groups disagreed among themselves about which form of government should be used, leading to civil war.

2. **Main Idea** People who made up the majority of the population did not have as many rights as some other people.

3. Baldwin and LaFontaine united voters into the Reform Party, which created laws that brought responsible government to the Province of Canada.

4. There were 23 years between the declaration of independence from Spain and independence from Haiti.

5. **Critical Thinking: *Compare and Contrast***
In Latin America, each country won its own independence from Spain, generally through violent revolutions. In Canada, Reformers united voters to use political means to resolve problems with Britain.

Write About History

1. Students' letters should reflect understanding of reasons why people struggle for independence. They should provide specific examples related to historic and/or modern-day events.

2. Students' editorials should be based on research and sound reasoning. They may wish to review guidelines for persuasive writing before they complete their editorials.

3. Before students write their reports, they might benefit from organizing their research into a flowchart, similar to the one used for the Fact File on PE p. 70.

Read on Your Own

Brazil, by Ann Heinrichs (Children's Press, ISBN 0-516-26164-9, 1997) **Easy**

Wars of Independence, by Richard Sanchez (Abdo & Daughters, ISBN 1-562-39334-0, 1994) **Easy**

The Boy with an R in His Hand, by James Reaney (The Porcupine's Quill, ISBN 0-889-84059-8, 1980) **On-Level**

Pioneer Girl, by Maryanne Caswell (Tundra Books, ISBN 0-887-76550-5, 2001) **On-Level**

The Dominican Republic, by Barbara Radcliffe Rogers and Lura Rogers (Children's Press, ISBN 0-516-21125-0, 1999) **Challenge**

A Pioneer Sampler: The Daily Life of a Pioneer Family in 1840, by Barbara Greenwood (Houghton Mifflin Company, ISBN 0-395-88393-8, 1998) **Challenge**

Nations in Conflict

Unit Overview

As civil war divided the United States, other countries in the Americas experienced power struggles. Canada found a peaceful resolution by forming a confederation. Mexico instituted social reforms. The borders of Paraguay, Argentina, and Brazil changed after the War of the Triple Alliance.

What I think will happen	What happened

Pupil Edition page 73

Draw a T-chart on the board and label the left column *What I think will happen* and the right column *What happened.* List the following facts on the board.

- Gold was discovered in British Columbia, Canada.
- Napoleon III, the French emperor, sent 30,000 troops to Mexico and conquered Mexico City. He made the Archduke of Austria the emperor of Mexico. Many Mexicans opposed this.
- Brazil, Argentina, and Uruguay formed a Triple Alliance in a war against Paraguay.

Have students work in small groups to predict what they think might have happened after each event listed on the board. As students study the unit, have them record in the *What happened* column what really happened. At the end of the unit review, let groups explain why they made the predictions they did and share the predictions they got right.

SOCIAL STUDIES
Background

About the Industrial Revolution

Tell students that the Industrial Revolution, which began in England, had a strong impact on Canada in the late 1800s. It transformed Montreal into the industrial capital of Canada.

- Factories in and around Montreal and Quebec City included saw mills, flour mills, distilleries, and iron smelters. Manufacturing soon became just as important for employment as farming.
- Between 1850 and 1871, Montreal's population increased from 50,000 to more than 100,000. Many British, French, and French Canadians moved to the area to work in the new factories.

SOCIAL STUDIES STRAND
Science • Technology

Steam Power

Improved transportation is one way in which science and technology have influenced the standard of living in North America.

- The invention of a practical steam engine in the 1700s marked a time of change in transportation. By the late 1800s, a steam locomotive could travel at 60 miles per hour. Trains moved goods and people long distances faster than ever before.
- Steamships took the place of sailing ships for transporting goods around the world. The growing availability of steamships and steam-powered trains made fare prices drop.

Additional Information

To establish guidelines for your students' safe and responsible use of the Internet, use the Scott Foresman Internet Guide.

Internet Links

To find out more about

- Canadian confederation, visit **www.nlc-bnc.ca** key words *John A. Macdonald*
- The Austrian emperor of Mexico, visit **www.si.edu** key word *Maximilian*
- Events in the United States at this time, visit **www.sfsocialstudies.com**

LESSON 1

Pupil Edition pages 74–77

Objectives

- Explain how George Brown, George Étienne Cartier, and John A. Macdonald made significant contributions to the development of Canada.
- Identify how improvements in transportation influenced the standard of living in Canada.
- Explain how differing assumptions that groups in Canada held regarding power, authority, and governance led people to support or oppose the Quebec Resolutions.

Vocabulary

sectionalism, p. 76; "Rep by Pop," p. 76; Great Coalition, p. 76; delegates, p. 76; Quebec Resolutions, p. 76

Quick Teaching Plan

If time is short, have pairs or groups of students prepare a debate in which students represent Canada East and Canada West.

- As they read the lesson, have students prepare a list of issues and arguments for each side.
- Have students debate the issues. Discuss why the two sides compromised and formed a united Canadian federation.

Canada Grows and Changes

1 Introduce and Motivate

Preview To activate prior knowledge, ask volunteers to fill in a word web on the board. Write *Forms of Transportation* in the center of the web. Have students suggest forms of transportation, and have volunteers record the suggestions. Then ask students to consider how long it took to transport goods and to travel before railroads existed. As students read Lesson 1, have them speculate on how life must have changed for people when railroads were built.

2 Teach and Discuss

Quick Summary The development of canals, railroads, and roads spurred economic growth in Canada. These changes in transportation made access to all of Canada easier. Debate soon developed about sectionalism versus confederation. With fears that the United States would try to expand into Canada, Canadians united and formed a confederation.

A Time of Change and Growth p. 75

- **Of the new canals, railroads, and roads, which do you think had the greatest impact on the lives of Canadians? Why do you think so?** Students should support their answers with details about the immediate goals of the construction. They should also consider other outcomes, such as job opportunities, ease of travel, and so on. **Express Ideas**

✔ **REVIEW ANSWER** The canals helped merchants move goods to market. This improved trade in Canada. As a result, Montreal and Quebec underwent rapid economic growth.
⊙ **Main Idea and Details**

The Conflict over Confederation p. 76

- **Why did Cartier favor strong local governments?** Cartier wanted strong local governments to protect French Canadians' language and customs. **Cause and Effect**

✔ **REVIEW ANSWER** George Brown wanted representation by population. George Étienne Cartier wanted strong local governments. John A. Macdonald wanted a central government.
⊙ **Main Idea and Details**

Canada Forms a Confederation p. 77

- **What do you think Canada would be like today if it had not unified into a confederacy?** Possible answers: Canada could have become two countries—Canada West and Canada East. Canada might be smaller because the United States might have expanded its borders. **Make Inferences**

✔ **REVIEW ANSWER** The advantages of confederation included the belief that the United States would not invade a unified Canada. The disadvantages of confederation included a fear that local governments would lose power to a central government.

⊙ **Main Idea and Details**

3 Close and Assess

Summarize the Lesson Begin an outline on the board. Use the lesson subheads for Roman numerals I, II, and III. Have students suggest important points to include under each subhead.

✔ **Lesson 1** **REVIEW**

1. ⊙ **Main Idea and Details**
   Details given should include system of canals built; railroads built; Douglas-Lillooet Road put in; united in a confederation

2. Possible answers: Created more jobs; made it easier to transport goods; allowed people to travel faster and farther

3. George Brown, George Étienne Cartier, and John A. Macdonald were the leaders of the Great Coalition. They worked together to make a plan that would unite Canada.

4. Canada West wanted a central government with representation by population, while Canada East wanted strong local governments. The provinces changed their views because civil war in the United States caused fear of expansion into Canada by the United States.

5. **Critical Thinking:** *Make Inferences* Possible answer: Canadians might not have hurried to confederation if they had not been afraid of possible expansion by the United States. French Canadians might have broken away to form their own government.

Link to ∞ **Culture** You may wish to introduce French words used in English, such as *etiquette, memoir, corps, coup, encore, café,* and *boulevard.* Students should describe a few differences between the two languages and pronounce and define at least two French words.

($) SOCIAL STUDIES STRAND
Economics

Free Trade

• Tell students that free-trade agreements between countries mean that governments do not regulate or interfere with trade between the trading partners.

• In 1854 Canada and the United States made their first free-trade agreement. The treaty opened fisheries both north and south of the border. It also provided for free trade in certain goods.

• Discuss with students how a free-trade agreement between the United States and Canada would help economic development. Lead students to see how the agreement opened new markets for both Canada and the United States.

READING STRATEGY
Main Idea and Details

In the Lesson Review, students complete a graphic organizer like the one below. You may want to provide students with a copy of Transparency 2 to complete as they read the lesson.

Main Idea and Details

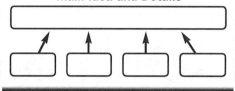

EXTEND LANGUAGE
ESL Support

Review Sequence Explain that order words can help students recognize the sequence of events.

Beginning Write on the board the following list of order words that show sequence of events: *first, next, last, then, second, finally,* and *after.* Discuss with students the meaning of each word. Then call on each student in the group to perform a simple task, such as sharpening a pencil. As each student performs the task, use sequence words to describe the action. For example, "First, Sasha sharpened his pencil. Next, Luisa sharpened her pencil," and so on. Repeat the activity, this time with students describing the sequence of events.

Intermediate Write events from the lesson on strips of paper. Include an order word in each sentence. Have students circle the clue order word in each and then put the strips in order.

Advanced Have students brainstorm a list of order words. Then ask students to use the words to write a short summary of the events in the lesson.

LESSON 2

Pupil Edition pages 78–81

Objectives

- Explain how Benito Juárez made significant contributions to the development of Mexico.
- Describe how political boundaries in Latin America have changed over time.
- Explain how differing assumptions regarding power, authority, and governance led to wars between Latin American countries.

Vocabulary

Gadsden Purchase, p. 79;

reformers, p. 79;

Triple Alliance, p. 80

Quick Teaching Plan

If time is short, have students write *Reform of Mexico* at the top of one paper and *War of the Triple Alliance* on another.

- Have students write the following headings on both papers: *Main Events, Causes,* and *Effects.*
- Have students read the lesson independently and record details under the appropriate headings.

Power Struggles in Latin America

1 Introduce and Motivate

Preview To activate prior knowledge, ask students to brainstorm a list of things they can do if they feel a rule or law is not fair. Tell students that as they read Lesson 2, they should think about what the citizens of Mexico did when they felt they were not being treated fairly.

2 Teach and Discuss

Quick Summary Reformers in Mexico, led by Benito Juárez, changed the constitution and made their country a democracy, but not without a fight. Francisco Solano López led Paraguay into a bloody war against a Triple Alliance (Uruguay, Argentina, and Brazil) over border disputes. Paraguay lost land and much of its population.

The Fight for Reform in Mexico p. 79

- **What was the main cause of the Mexican civil war in 1858?** Reformers wanted many new laws, fair trials for all, land reforms to help the poor, and a new constitution. Some people strongly opposed these rapid changes. **Cause and Effect**

✓ **REVIEW ANSWER** Many Mexicans were angry at Santa Anna for the Gadsden Purchase, and they blamed him for losing the war against the United States. Juárez wanted laws that treated people fairly. When the French ruled Mexico, Juárez fought to have a leader who treated Mexicans fairly. **Cause and Effect**

A War over Borders p. 80

- **Do you think that Francisco Solano López should have continued fighting when his troops were outnumbered? Why or why not?** Possible answers: Yes, because he did not want to give up. No, because too many people were killed. **Express Ideas**

✓ **REVIEW ANSWER** Some causes of the war included Paraguay's border disputes with Brazil, Argentina, and Uruguay; Brazil would not pay tariffs to Paraguay; Argentina did not let Paraguayan troops cross its borders; and Paraguayans were afraid they would not be able to use the Río de la Plata for trade. **Cause and Effect**

Results of the War p. 81

- **Compare and contrast Benito Juárez with Francisco Solano López.** Possible answers: Both led countries and both led armies in war. Juárez wanted to help all people of Mexico, including the poor. When Juárez was president, he made Mexico stronger. López led his country into a terrible war. After the war, Paraguay was left smaller and weaker. **Compare and Contrast**

✓ **REVIEW ANSWER** The boundary dispute was settled and Brazil and Argentina both received land from Paraguay. The Brazilian army occupied Paraguay for six years. ⊙ **Main Idea and Details**

3 Close and Assess

Summarize the Lesson Have students write *Benito Juárez, Paraguay,* and *Triple Alliance* on index cards. On separate cards, have students write three facts about each topic. Have students shuffle the fact cards and then match them to the correct topic cards.

✓ Lesson 2 REVIEW

1. ⊙ **Main Idea and Details**

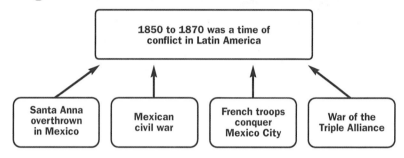

1850 to 1870 was a time of conflict in Latin America

Santa Anna overthrown in Mexico

Mexican civil war

French troops conquer Mexico City

War of the Triple Alliance

2. Benito Juárez and the reformers wanted laws that would treat all citizens fairly, grant fair trials for all, and bring about land reforms to help the poor.

3. López thought Argentina would support him. He thought Uruguayans would want his help.

4. Paraguay gave up land to both Brazil and Argentina.

5. Critical Thinking: *Evaluate* Answers will vary but must be supported by facts from the text.

 **Link to ⚭ Mathematics** About 150,000 Paraguayans died in the war. There were about 470,000 more American soldiers who died in the United States Civil War than Paraguayans who died in the War of the Triple Alliance.

 THEN AND NOW
Cinco de Mayo

Why is Cinco de Mayo an important Mexican holiday? Possible answer: It is inspiring for the Mexican people to know that they were able to defeat a bigger and better-equipped army that was invading their land. **Evaluate**

READING STRATEGY
Main Idea and Details

In the Lesson Review, students complete a graphic organizer like the one below. You may want to provide students with a copy of Transparency 2 to complete as they read the lesson.

Main Idea and Details

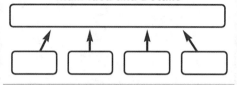
MEETING INDIVIDUAL NEEDS
Leveled Practice

Make a Speech Ask students to assume the role of Benito Juárez convincing the Mexican people that their government must change.

Easy Students should include two examples from the lesson of the kinds of changes that should be made to Mexican laws. **Reteach**

On-Level Students should describe former government leaders and why they were not good for Mexico, as well as describe needed changes to the Mexican constitution. **Extend**

Challenge Students should write a campaign speech for Juárez that uses historical facts and reformers' opinions to convince the people of Mexico that Juárez would be the best president for them. If time allows, you may also have students design campaign posters. **Enrich**

CURRICULUM CONNECTION
Art

Draw a Political Cartoon

• Help students brainstorm a list of current events that might be good subjects for political cartoons.

• Have students create their own political cartoons based on current events. Display the cartoons and encourage students to try to explain the cartoons of others.

Write the Essay

Plan and Prewrite

You may wish to have students use the documents in this unit to write an essay about conflicts that occur in or between nations. Discuss the topic and share with students the rubric that will be used to score their essays (see TE p. 61). Have students review the documents and the answers they recorded on their DBQ Record Sheets.

Page 75, song: The Canadian miners had a friendly rivalry with the miners from the United States.

Page 79, cartoon: Possible answer: It shows that as Napoleon III tries to control Mexico, he is headed straight for a cliff, or defeat.

Page 79, quotation: Possible answer: Because some groups did not show respect for others, there could be no peace.

Page 80, map: Paraguay's borders grew smaller. Paraguay lost land to Brazil and Argentina.

Page 81, time line: 4 years

Page 83, cartoon: Possible answer: The United States is an unstoppable engine that will run over anything in its way.

Discuss Before students begin planning their essays, you may wish to have a class discussion to stimulate students' thinking. Ask students to identify some different reasons for conflicts in or between nations. Remind students that the unit provides the historical context for their responses.

Use a Graphic Organizer Remind students that a prewriting tool such as a graphic organizer will help them write a better essay. Model on the board a web diagram.

Suggest that students complete the graphic organizer with information from the documents. For example, students could use this diagram to list the types of conflicts that occurred in the nations they learned about in Unit 7.

Tell students they may use other kinds of organizers, as long as the organizers are suited to the topic. Once students complete their prewriting, have them write first drafts of their essays.

Content Tips Point out that conflicts between two nations or governments do not necessarily mean conflicts exist between individual citizens of those countries. For example, the folk song suggests that Canadian miners had a good-natured rivalry with miners who arrived from the United States.

National and International Conflicts

Evaluate and Revise

Check Content Once students have completed their first drafts, provide the following checklist to assist them in evaluating what they have written:

❑ Have I used information from the documents to draw my conclusion?

❑ Have I shown how ideas or information from each document are related to the topic?

❑ Have I included my own thoughts in the essay?

❑ Have I avoided simply summarizing the documents?

❑ Is my point clearly stated and explained?

❑ Is my essay logically organized?

❑ Do I use appropriate details to support my topic sentences?

❑ Have I avoided including statements that are unrelated to the topic?

Proofread After they have edited their essays for content, remind students to use a standard proofreading checklist to look for errors in spelling, grammar, and mechanics. Then have them write and submit the final drafts of their essays.

Score the Essay You may wish to use the rubric at right to score students' essays. If you have emphasized particular thinking or writing strategies during the study of Unit 7, you may wish to modify the rubric to include those skills.

Scoring Rubric
Unit 7 Document-Based Essay

4
- Shows superior understanding of the topic.
- Relates each document to the topic of national or international conflicts.
- Includes numerous insights (conclusions, inferences) that are well explained and supported by the documents.
- Includes no factual or mechanical errors.

3
- Shows reasonable understanding of the topic.
- Relates most of the documents to the topic of national or international conflicts.
- Includes some insights (conclusions, inferences) that are clear and for the most part supported by the document.
- Includes very few factual or mechanical errors.

2
- Shows minimal understanding of the topic.
- Attempts to relate some documents to the topic of national or international conflicts.
- Includes description, quotes, or paraphrasing, but no insights (conclusions, inferences) into the topic.
- Includes a number of factual or mechanical errors.

1
- Shows little or no understanding of the topic.
- Does not attempt to relate documents to the topic of national or international conflicts.
- Includes only vague references, if any, to content of the documents.
- Includes many factual or mechanical errors.

0
- Uses no accurate data, or response is totally unrelated to the topic.
- Is either illegible or incoherent, and no sense can be made of the response.
- Paper is blank.

Pupil Edition page 84

Vocabulary and People

Sample answers:

1. John A. Macdonald helped form the Great Coalition and helped write a plan that united Canada as a confederation.

2. Leaders who represented different interests formed the Great Coalition and worked together to unite Canada as a confederation.

3. The Quebec Resolutions were the first step in uniting Canada.

4. The Gadsden Purchase was the sale by Mexico of La Mesilla Valley to the United States.

5. Reformers are people who want change. In Mexico the reformers wanted fair laws, so they overthrew Santa Anna.

6. As president of Mexico, Benito Juárez developed the Mexican economy and instituted social reforms.

7. The Triple Alliance was an alliance of three countries, Brazil, Argentina, and Uruguay. These three fought against and eventually defeated Paraguay. After the war, Brazil and Argentina received land from Paraguay.

Facts and Main Ideas

Sample answers:

1. The discovery of gold made people want to travel to the west, which led to the building of important roads.

2. **Main Idea** Canadians had representatives of each area debate the pros and cons of uniting. The representatives found that they were united against expansion into Canada by the United States.

3. The reformers struggled first with Santa Anna and then with the French for control of Mexico.

4. **Main Idea** Brazil would not pay trade tariffs to Paraguay, and Paraguay feared Brazil and Argentina would cut off access to the Río de la Plata, an important transport route.

5. **Critical Thinking: *Compare and Contrast*** Mexico resolved political differences with war, while Canada had representatives of differing opinions debate. Both countries resolved their problems with new constitutions that created democracies.

Write About History

1. Students' letters should describe the journey to British Columbia, the other miners, and the new roads being built.

2. Students' speeches should include details from the text as part of their arguments.

3. Students' biographies should include three or more details from the life of Benito Juárez or one of the Great Coalition leaders. The paper should flow in chronological order.

Read on Your Own

Benito Juárez: President of Mexico, by Frank De Varona (Millbrook Press, ISBN 1-562-94807-5, 1994) **Easy**

The Railroad, by Bobbie Kalman (Crabtree, ISBN 0-778-70076-3, 1999) **Easy**

Argentina, Chile, Paraguay, Uruguay, by Anna Selby (Raintree/Steck Vaughn, ISBN 0-817-25408-0, 1999) **On-Level**

Sylvia Stark: A Pioneer, by Ernest Jones and Victoria Scott (Open Hand Publishing, ISBN 0-940-88038-5, 1992) **On-Level**

Paraguay in Pictures, by Nathan A. Haverstock (Lerner Publications Company, ISBN 0-822-51819-8, 1995) **Challenge**

A Pioneer Sampler: The Daily Life of a Pioneer Family in 1840, by Barbara Greenwood (Houghton Mifflin, ISBN 0-395-88393-8, 1998) **Challenge**

Expansion and Change in the Americas

Unit Overview

In the late 1800s, millions of immigrants from Europe and Asia arrived in the Americas. In Canada, as in the United States, railroad companies hired immigrant workers to build a transcontinental railroad. European immigrants started farms on lands in western Canada. In Latin America, as in the United States, immigrants from Europe arrived in cities to find jobs.

Draw a web diagram on the board. Ask students to recall what they know about immigrant experiences in the United States.

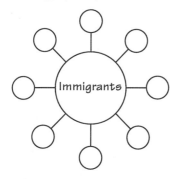

Students should include reasons why immigrants came, where they settled, and what kinds of jobs they did. Record students' ideas in the diagram. As students read Unit 8, ask them to create similar web diagrams to record information about immigrant experiences in Canada and Latin America.

 **SOCIAL STUDIES**
Background

Science and Technology

Share the following information with students:

- Exchanges of technologies between nations of the Americas and Europe have changed life in these regions. Ferdinand Carré invented a refrigeration system in France in the late 1800s. In 1877 Carré designed a system for the *Paraguay,* the world's first refrigerated ship. This ship carried frozen beef from Argentina to France. Refrigerated ships made it possible for perishable items to travel to distant places around the world.

- Science and technology have also played an important role in North America. The building of the transcontinental railroad aided the economic growth of western Canada. Free land attracted settlers. Improved farming methods made Manitoba an important wheat-growing area. When worldwide demand for wheat increased, the western provinces grew into a prosperous region.

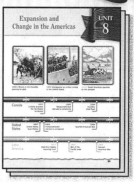

Pupil Edition page 85

 ## Additional Information

⚠️ *To establish guidelines for your students' safe and responsible use of the Internet, use the Scott Foresman Internet Guide.*

Internet Links

To find out more about

- The Métis, visit **www.nlc-bnc.ca** key words *Louis Riel*
- Cuba's independence from Spain, visit **www.loc.gov** key words *Spanish-American War*
- Events in the United States at this time, visit **www.sfsocialstudies.com**

LESSON 1

Pupil Edition pages 86–89

Objectives

- Describe the expansion of Canada in the late 1800s.
- Explain how the completion of the transcontinental railroad brought changes in western Canada.
- List reasons why people from other countries settled in western Canada in the late 1800s.

Vocabulary

British North America Act, p. 87; dominion, p. 87; Canadian Pacific Railway Company, p. 88

Quick Teaching Plan

If time is short, have students create annotated maps.

- Provide each student with an outline map of Canada.
- As students read Lesson 1 independently, have them locate and label places mentioned in the text.
- Have students write key facts next to each place they have labeled.

Canada Expands From Sea to Sea

1 Introduce and Motivate

Preview To activate prior knowledge, ask students to describe how the United States expanded during the late 1800s. Tell students that in Lesson 1 they will learn how Canada expanded to the Pacific coast.

2 Teach and Discuss

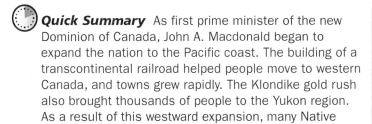

Quick Summary As first prime minister of the new Dominion of Canada, John A. Macdonald began to expand the nation to the Pacific coast. The building of a transcontinental railroad helped people move to western Canada, and towns grew rapidly. The Klondike gold rush also brought thousands of people to the Yukon region. As a result of this westward expansion, many Native Americans signed treaties that gave their land to the government.

Growth of a New Nation   p. 87

- **How do you think the British North America Act affected Canadians' view of themselves?** Since the British North America Act gave Canada more independence, Canadians may have felt they had more freedom. Canadians may also have felt they now had more say in how to run their country. **Make Inferences**

✓ **REVIEW ANSWER** Louis Riel led a Métis rebellion. Part of Rupert's Land became Manitoba. The government set aside land for the Métis. ☺ **Sequence**

Railroads Link Canada   p. 88

- **How do you think the technology of building a transcontinental railroad influenced the standard of living in Canada?** Possible answer: It probably improved the standard of living for landowners because buying and selling land became big business. It also made it easier for people to move from one part of the country to another and probably opened up new job opportunities. **Make Inferences**

✓ **REVIEW ANSWER** Many Native Americans moved to reservations. **Cause and Effect**

Settlement of the West   p. 89

- **How do you think the Canadian Pacific Railway Company (CPR) played a role in bringing new cultures to Canada?** In order to sell land to settlers, the CPR attracted settlers from Europe. These groups of settlers brought their own cultures to Canada. **Apply Information**

✔ **REVIEW ANSWER** News of the discovery spread to other countries. Thousands of people came to the Yukon.
⊙ **Sequence**

C SOCIAL STUDIES STRAND
Culture

Learning About Cultural Groups

- Explain to students that the world is made up of cultural groups that have distinctive ways of life. Cultural groups might include people of the same ethnic heritage, people sent to represent a nation, members of a religious group, and so on. Characteristics such as language, beliefs, economic activities, land-use practices, education systems, traditional customs, and holidays help define a cultural group.

- As cultural groups migrate throughout the world, they come into contact with other groups and adopt other characteristics. This process creates complex cultures. Cultural groups that have migrated to Canada and Latin America have contributed to the cultures of those countries. For example, Tibetans who have migrated to Canada have shared their custom of traditional dances. Italian immigrants to Brazil have shared their language—*ciao,* an Italian word for "goodbye," has become *tchau,* a common farewell in Brazil.

3 Close and Assess

Summarize the Lesson Have students use the entries for Canada on the time line on PE p. 89 as the start of a summary of the main ideas of the lesson. For each time-line entry, students should add a few important facts to round out the summary.

✔ **Lesson 1** REVIEW

1. ⊙ **Sequence**
   1870: Part of Rupert's Land became the province of Manitoba.
   1871: British Columbia agreed to join the Dominion.
   1885: Transcontinental railroad was completed.
   1898: A gold rush brought thousands of miners to the Yukon.

2. Native Americans moved to reservations. Towns grew rapidly. Buying and selling land became big business.

3. The CPR received millions of acres of land for building the railroad. It wanted to sell that land to settlers.

4. They came to get low-cost land or to search for gold.

5. **Critical Thinking:** *Draw Conclusions* The Métis feared the government would take away their land and change their way of life. Some people felt that the offer of land would attract greedy people instead of hardworking settlers.

Link to ⚭ **Economics** Students' flowcharts should include transportation of raw materials to factories and finished goods to markets.

READING STRATEGY
Sequence

In the Lesson Review, students complete a graphic organizer like the one below. You may want to provide students with a copy of Transparency 10 to complete as they read the lesson.

Sequence

```
┌─────────────────────────┐
│                         │
└─────────────────────────┘
            │
            ▼
┌─────────────────────────┐
│                         │
└─────────────────────────┘
            │
            ▼
┌─────────────────────────┐
│                         │
└─────────────────────────┘
            │
            ▼
┌─────────────────────────┐
│                         │
└─────────────────────────┘
```

EXTEND LANGUAGE
ESL Support

Demonstrate Understanding of Meaning Help students understand words related to railroad transportation.

Beginning Use the photograph on p. 88 to help students understand the meaning of the following words used in the text: *track*, *rails*, and *spike*. Have students point to the corresponding object as you say the words out loud.

Intermediate Help students list a sequence of steps in building a railroad. Have them use the terms presented in the text.

Advanced Help students make a list of words related to railroad transportation today. These may include *commuter*, *ticket*, *schedule*, and *freight*.

LESSON 2

Pupil Edition pages 90–93

Objectives

- Explain how European immigrants brought their ideas and ways of life to Latin American cities in the late 1800s.
- Explain the effect of supply and demand on expansion of Latin American trade.
- Describe the changes in political boundaries that resulted from wars in Latin America in the late 1800s.

Vocabulary

refrigerator ship, p. 92; Spanish-American War, p. 93

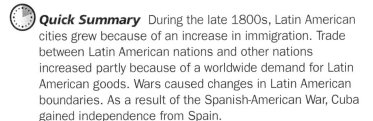 **Quick** Teaching Plan

If time is short, have students read the lesson independently, looking for causes and effects of changes in Latin America in the late 1800s.

- Have students create a cause-and-effect chart to show the changes brought about by an increase in immigration, an expansion of trade, and wars.

Changes in Latin America

1 Introduce and Motivate

Preview To activate prior knowledge, have students brainstorm a list of ways the United States changed in the late 1800s. Ask volunteers to record ideas on the board. Then tell students that they will learn ways in which Latin America changed during that time as they read Lesson 2.

2 Teach and Discuss

Quick Summary During the late 1800s, Latin American cities grew because of an increase in immigration. Trade between Latin American nations and other nations increased partly because of a worldwide demand for Latin American goods. Wars caused changes in Latin American boundaries. As a result of the Spanish-American War, Cuba gained independence from Spain.

Increase in Immigration   p. 91

- **Why do you think most immigrants to Latin America in the late 1800s ended up in cities?** Possible answer: There were more jobs in the cities. **Draw Conclusions**

✓ **REVIEW ANSWER** Farmers grew crops or worked on plantations. Immigrants in cities worked as clerks, craftspersons, or laborers. **Main Idea and Details**

Expansion of Trade   p. 92

- **How was economic growth in Latin America related to industrial development in the United States?** The growing automobile industry in the United States created a market for Latin American resources such as rubber, which led to economic growth in Latin America. **Cause and Effect**

✓ **REVIEW ANSWER** The refrigerator ship made it possible to export beef from Argentina to Europe, which increased trade between Latin America and Europe. **Cause and Effect**

Results of War   p. 93

- **How did the Conquest of the Desert affect westward migration and expansion in Argentina?** Argentina took over Native American lands in the west, which opened these lands to settlers for farming and ranching. **Cause and Effect**

✓ **REVIEW ANSWER** José Martí led a revolution against Spanish rule. The United States came to Cuba's aid and defeated Spanish forces. As a result of the Spanish-American War, Cuba gained independence from Spain. **Sequence**

3 Close and Assess

Summarize the Lesson Have students write a question for each subhead in the lesson. Then have them exchange questions with a partner and summarize the lesson by writing an answer to each question.

✓ Lesson 2 REVIEW

1. ⊙ **Sequence**
   Refrigerator ships carry beef from Argentina to Europe <u>1877</u>
   Bolivia loses coastal lands <u>1884</u>
   Central Railway is completed in Peru <u>1893</u>
   Cuba becomes independent from Spain <u>1898</u>

2. Immigrants from Europe came to Latin America to seek a better life. Some farmed or worked on plantations. Others went to cities to find jobs.

3. A worldwide demand for goods from Latin American farms and mines caused an expansion of trade between Latin America and other countries.

4. Bolivia lost its coastal lands, which affected its trade because it had no ports.

5. **Critical Thinking: *Cause and Effect*** Cities reflected the languages, customs, and ideas of the people who settled there. As immigration increased, so did the cultural complexity of the cities.

Link to ∞ Language Arts Students might use the Internet or other library resources to find the meanings of Latin American place names. Other examples include Rio de Janeiro, which means "river of January," and Puerto Rico, which means "rich harbor."

FACT FILE

Latin American Cowboys

Cowboy ways of life are examples of social and cultural exchanges between peoples of Latin America and the United States. Some Mexican cowboys (vaqueros) remained in Texas after Texas declared independence from Mexico. People from the eastern United States who headed west to work on ranches learned skills from the vaqueros.

- **What did cowboys in the United States learn from Latin American cowboys?** They learned skills such as roping and riding. They also wore clothing similar to that of cowboys in Latin America. **Main Idea and Details**

READING STRATEGY
Sequence

In the Lesson Review, students complete a Sequence graphic organizer. You may want to provide students with a copy of Transparency 10 to complete as they read the lesson. This graphic organizer can be seen on p. 93 of the PE.

MEETING INDIVIDUAL NEEDS
Leveled Practice

Understand Economic Concepts
Lead a brief discussion about why it is important to understand economic concepts. Point out that economics played a key role in the expansion of Latin America.

Easy Write the following terms on the board: *resources*, *markets*, and *supply and demand*. Help students write a definition for each term. Then have them use each term in a sentence about Latin American economies in the late 1800s. **Reteach**

On-Level Ask students to explain how supply and demand affects the price of goods. Ask what happens to price if the supply is higher than the demand. (Price goes down.) Ask what happens to price if the demand is higher than the supply. (Price goes up.) **Extend**

Challenge Have students work in small groups to create diagrams showing how supply and demand affected the market for Latin American resources in the late 1800s. **Enrich**

CURRICULUM CONNECTION
Music

Latin American Music
The music of Latin America reflects the different cultures of its people.

- Have students use library or online resources to research and listen to Latin American music. Categories include tango, samba, merengue, salsa, and mariachi.
- Discuss ways that Latin American music has influenced music in the United States.

Write the Essay

Plan and Prewrite

Read aloud the sentence on PE p. 95 stating the topic for the document-based question essay. Discuss the topic and share with students the rubric by which their essays will be scored (see TE p. 69). Have students review the documents and their answers to the related questions.

Page 87, map: Canada acquired Ontario, Quebec, New Brunswick, and Nova Scotia first. The two territories are Yukon Territory and Northwest Territories.

Page 88, quote: The bishop thought that many greedy people would view Manitoba as a place to gain wealth without having to work for it.

Page 89, chart: Because many people went to the Yukon Territory during the gold rush, cities and transportation developed.

Page 91, quote: The people who immigrated to Buenos Aires were from many different countries and cultures.

Page 91, photo: Because there were more people in Buenos Aires, the cities were probably busier. There was probably more traffic.

Page 92, map: Possible answer: Immigrants may have come to Latin America to work in jobs that produced goods for export, such as coffee, copper, or rubber.

Discuss Before students begin planning their essays, you may wish to have a class discussion to stimulate students' thinking. Ask students how the documents are related to immigration in Canada and Latin America in the late 1800s. Remind students that the unit provides the historical context for their responses.

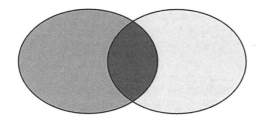

Use a Graphic Organizer Remind students that a prewriting tool such as a graphic organizer will help them write a better essay. Help students create a Venn diagram to compare and contrast immigration in Canada and Latin America. Tell students they may use other kinds of organizers, as long as the organizers are suited to the topic. Once students complete their prewriting, have them write first drafts of their essays.

Content Tips Encourage students to use higher-level thinking strategies as they review the documents. Students may draw conclusions about reasons for immigration to Canada and Latin America, or they may make inferences about the new opportunities and challenges immigrants faced in their new homelands. Remind students that any conclusions or inferences should be based on the facts presented in the documents.

Evaluate and Revise

Check Content After students have completed their first drafts, provide the following checklist to assist them in evaluating what they have written:

❏ Have I used information from the documents to draw my conclusion?

❏ Have I shown how information or ideas from each document are related to the topic?

❏ Have I included my own thoughts in the essay?

❏ Have I avoided simply summarizing the documents?

❏ Is my point clearly stated and explained?

❏ Is my essay logically organized?

❏ Do I use appropriate details to support my topic sentences?

❏ Have I avoided including statements that are unrelated to the topic?

Proofread After they have edited their essays for content, remind students to use a standard proofreading checklist to look for errors in spelling, grammar, and mechanics. Then have them write and submit the final drafts of their essays.

Score the Essay You may wish to use the rubric at right to score students' essays. If you have emphasized particular thinking or writing strategies during the study of Unit 8, you may wish to modify the rubric to include those skills.

Scoring Rubric
Unit 8 Document-Based Essay

4	• Shows superior understanding of the topic. • Relates each document to the topic of immigration. • Includes numerous insights (conclusions, inferences) that are well explained and supported by the documents. • Includes no factual or mechanical errors.
3	• Shows reasonable understanding of the topic. • Relates most of the documents to the topic of immigration. • Includes some insights (conclusions, inferences) that are clear and for the most part supported by the document. • Includes very few factual or mechanical errors.
2	• Shows minimal understanding of the topic. • Attempts to relate some documents to the topic of immigration. • Includes description, quotes, or paraphrasing, but no insights (conclusions, inferences, analysis, evaluations) into the topic. • Includes a number of factual or mechanical errors.
1	• Shows little or no understanding of the topic. • Does not attempt to relate documents to the topic of immigration. • Includes only vague references, if any, to content of the documents. • Includes many factual or mechanical errors.
0	• Uses no accurate data, or response is totally unrelated to the topic. • Is either illegible or incoherent, and no sense can be made of the response. • Paper is blank.

Pupil Edition page 96

Vocabulary, People, and Places

Sample answers:

1. Rupert's Land was a large territory in northern and western Canada that Macdonald bought from the Hudson's Bay Company.

2. Louis Riel was a Métis leader who headed a rebellion to protest the sale of Rupert's Land.

3. The Canadian Pacific Railway Company completed the transcontinental railroad in Canada.

4. The Klondike is a region in the Yukon Territory where gold was discovered in 1896.

5. José Martí was a poet and freedom fighter who led a revolution against Spanish rule in Cuba.

6. The Spanish-American War was a conflict between Spain and the United States in 1898 that resulted in freedom for Cuba.

Facts and Main Ideas

Sample answers:

1. Canada bought Rupert's Land from the Hudson's Bay Company.

2. **Main Idea** The Métis who lived in Rupert's Land feared that the Canadian government would take away their land and change their way of life.

3. Because of increased trade, Latin American farms and mines produced more goods to export.

4. **Main Idea** In the War of the Pacific, Peru lost mineral-rich lands, and Bolivia lost its coastal lands. In the Conquest of the Desert, Argentina took over Native American lands. As a result of the Spanish-American War, Spain gave up claims to Cuba.

5. The Spanish-American War affected both the United States and Latin America.

6. **Critical Thinking: *Compare and Contrast*** Both Canada and Latin America experienced boundary changes, improvements in railroad transportation, and increased immigration. Canada expanded by acquiring new lands. Latin America expanded trade.

Write About History

1. Students' advertisements should reflect understanding of reasons why Europeans might want to settle in Canada and opportunities that Canada had to offer.

2. Students' reports might include the effect of improved transportation on settlement as well as on trade.

3. Students' biographies should include accomplishments of each man. You might have students work in pairs to construct Venn diagrams comparing Riel and Martí.

Read on Your Own

Argentina: The People, by Bobbie Kalman and Greg Nickles (Crabtree Publishing, ISBN 0-865-05245-X, 2000) **Easy**

Sarah and the People of Sand River, by W.D. Valgardson (Groundwood Books, ISBN 0-888-99255-6, 1996) **Easy**

Spanish-American War, by Kathlyn Gay and Martin Gay (Twenty First Century Books, ISBN 0-805-02847-1, 1997) **On-Level**

Ultimate Field Trip 4: A Week in the 1800s, by Susan E. Goodman (Atheneum, ISBN 0-689-83045-9, 2000) **On-Level**

Gold Rush Fever: A Story of the Klondike, 1898, by Barbara Greenwood (Kids Can Press, ISBN 1-550-74850-5, 2001) **Challenge**

José Martí: Cuban Patriot and Poet, by David Goodnough (Enslow Publishers Inc., ISBN 0-894-90761-1, 1996) **Challenge**

Canada and Latin America in the 1900s

Unit Overview

During the 1900s, Canada and the countries of Latin America became increasingly involved in world events. Like the United States, Canada fought in wars and joined the United Nations to promote world peace and understanding. Many Latin American nations established democratic governments and participated in the Organization of American States to provide peaceful settlement of conflicts. The nations of the Americas became economically interdependent.

Pupil Edition page 97

	Accomplishments	Challenges
United States		
Canada		
Latin America		

On the board, draw a chart like the one above. Ask students to recall some accomplishments of the United States during the 1900s. Then ask them to describe some challenges that faced the United States. List their responses on the chart. As students read Unit 9, ask them to note accomplishments and challenges for Canada and Latin America during the 1900s. Call on volunteers to add their answers to the chart.

SOCIAL STUDIES
Background

About International Relations

Share the following information with students:

- Canada and the countries of Latin America belong to organizations that work to fight hunger, diseases, and ignorance and to promote peace and cultural understanding.
- Canadians have played an important role in the history of the United Nations. A Canadian was the main author of the Universal Declaration of Human Rights. Another Canadian won the Nobel Peace Prize for his work in helping to bring peace to Egypt during the Suez Crisis of 1956.
- Thirty-five American countries belong to the Organization of American States. The OAS was formed in 1948, but it was not a new idea. As far back as 1826 Simón Bolívar had hoped to form an organization of states in the Western Hemisphere. Cuba is a member of the OAS but is not permitted to vote or participate in activities because it is a Communist dictatorship, as well as due to its involvement in the Cuban Missile Crisis.

About the Panama Canal

- Explain to students that the building of the Panama Canal provides examples of how science and technology have influenced the standard of living in Central America. The United States paid Panama for the right to build the canal. The construction also provided jobs in Panama. Army doctors controlled yellow fever, a deadly disease carried by mosquitoes in Panama.

Additional Information

⚠️ *To establish guidelines for your students' safe and responsible use of the Internet, use the Scott Foresman Internet Guide.*

Internet Links

To find out more about

- Nunavut, visit **www.nunavut.com** key words *Inuit tradition, Nunavut government*
- Panama Canal, visit **memory.loc.gov** key words *Panama Canal*
- Events in the United States at this time, visit **www.sfsocialstudies.com**

Pupil Edition pages 98–101

Objectives

- Describe how Canada has made progress toward unity while protecting the individual rights of its peoples.
- Summarize the economic decisions that affected the exchange of goods and services between Canada and the United States.
- Discuss the role of natural resources in Canada's concerns for the future.

Vocabulary

Inuit, p. 99; **separatism,** p. 99; **Canada Act,** p. 99; **St. Lawrence Seaway,** p. 100; **North American Free Trade Agreement,** p. 100

Quick Teaching Plan

If time is short, have students read *Focus on the Main Idea* on p. 98. Ask them to write at least three questions related to the main idea.

- As students read Lesson 1 independently, have them take notes that will help them answer the questions.
- After reading, have students share their questions and answers with the class.

Canada and the World

1 Introduce and Motivate

Preview To activate prior knowledge, ask students what people mean when they say, "It's a small world." (Possible answer: There are many connections among nations and peoples of the world.) Tell students that as they read Lesson 1, they will learn about connections between Canada and the world.

2 Teach and Discuss

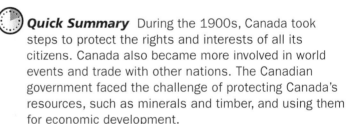

Quick Summary During the 1900s, Canada took steps to protect the rights and interests of all its citizens. Canada also became more involved in world events and trade with other nations. The Canadian government faced the challenge of protecting Canada's resources, such as minerals and timber, and using them for economic development.

Problems and Progress in Canada
p. 99

- **In what way is the government of Canada like that of the United States?** Both governments have constitutions that protect the rights of citizens, maintain order, and provide security. **Compare and Contrast**

✓ **REVIEW ANSWER** The Inuit wanted to regain control of their traditional lands. The Canadian government agreed to give the Inuit a vast region of the Northwest Territories. The territory of Nunavut was created in 1999. ☺ **Summarize**

SOCIAL STUDIES STRAND
Government

- Point out that the governments of the United States, Canada, and Latin American countries share some similarities, but they also differ in structure and function.
- Tell students that just as state governments within the United States differ from one another, governments of provinces and territories within Canada differ from one another. For example, the territory of Nunavut has government leaders who address the needs of the Inuit.
- Explain that Canada, like the United States, has a democratic government. Most Latin American nations now have democratic governments. Cuba has the only Communist government in Latin America.
- Explain that the constitutions of different nations in the Western Hemisphere differ in many details, but they are used to set down rules on such issues as the organization of government and the powers of different branches of government. They can also define the rights and responsibilities of citizens, such as who is allowed to vote and whether they must vote.

Canada's Involvement in World Events
p. 100

- **How do you think the North American Free Trade Agreement promotes economic growth and development among nations in North America?** Possible answer: Because NAFTA did away with tariffs, or taxes on imported goods, it made selling some goods in foreign markets more practical and profitable. **Apply Information**

✓ **REVIEW ANSWER** Canada exports goods to many countries. It also imports goods from the United States. ☉ **Summarize**

Canada's Concerns for the Future
p. 101

- **Do you think it is possible to both protect and develop natural resources? What are some ways people try to protect natural resources?** Students should recognize that the possibility of both developing and protecting natural resources is different for different resources. **Express Ideas**

✓ **REVIEW ANSWER** Canada is a leading producer of copper, gold, iron, and timber. Government programs seek ways to protect these resources and make the best use of them for Canada's economic development. ☉ **Summarize**

3 Close and Assess

Summarize the Lesson List the subheads from this lesson on the board. Call on students to identify one main idea and one detail for each subhead.

✓ **Lesson 1** **REVIEW**

1. ☉ **Summarize**
   [Detail 1] The Charter of Rights and Freedoms guarantees justice and equal rights for all citizens.
   [Detail 2] French and English were made official languages.
   [Detail 3] Nunavut was created as a homeland for the Inuit.

2. Traditional Inuit ways of life include the skills needed to hunt and fish in the Arctic. Some Inuit groups celebrate a spring festival with a blanket toss.

3. Canada worked with the United States to build the St. Lawrence Seaway. This increased trade for both nations. In 1989 Canada and the United States signed an agreement that did away with tariffs. In 1994 Canada signed NAFTA, which allows it to trade freely with Mexico and the United States.

4. Canada's natural resources are important to its economy.

5. **Critical Thinking:** *Express Ideas* Possible answer: Canada and the United States are among the largest and most powerful nations in the world. They also share a long border. A good relationship between them helps keep peace throughout the world, strengthens trade, and helps build a strong world economy.

Link to ∞ **Art** Students' posters and explanations should reflect Canada's people, land, and resources.

READING STRATEGY
Summarize

In the Lesson Review, students complete a graphic organizer like the one below. You might want to provide students with a copy of Transparency 6 to complete as they review the lesson.

Summarize

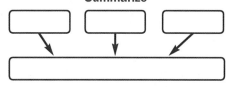

MEETING INDIVIDUAL NEEDS
Learning Styles

Describe Canada in the 1900s
Using their individual learning styles, students review key events in Canada during the 1900s.

Visual Learning Ask students to make an illustrated time line of key events in Canada from 1914 to 1999.

Verbal Learning Have students work in groups and give short oral summaries of each subhead in Lesson 1.

Pupil Edition pages 102–105

Objectives

- Describe the role of governments in Latin America today.
- Summarize ways that international organizations brought about changes in Latin America.
- Explain how the types and availability of resources are important to economic development in Latin America today.

Vocabulary

Organization of American States (OAS), p. 104; deforestation, p. 105; indigenous peoples, p. 105

**Quick Teaching Plan**

If time is short, have students create an annotated time line.

- As students read the lesson independently, have them make a list of important dates and details.
- Have students use their notes to make a time line with annotations about important events.
- Discuss the completed time lines.

Latin America and the World

1 Introduce and Motivate

Preview To activate prior knowledge, ask students to list some rights people enjoy as citizens of the United States. Tell students that as they read Lesson 2, they will learn how citizens of Latin American countries gained rights.

2 Teach and Discuss

Quick Summary During the 1900s, people in many Latin American countries established democratic governments with constitutions that protect their rights. International organizations formed to help maintain peace and aid economic development in Latin America. Protection and development of natural resources are continuing concerns for Latin American nations.

New Governments   p. 103

- **Citizens of different countries in Latin America do not all have the same rights. How are the rights of citizens in the United States similar to or different from those of citizens in Latin American countries?** Similar: Like the United States, some Latin American countries have constitutions that support justice, due process, equality, majority rule, and minority rights. Different: People in the United States can own land and businesses. In Cuba only the government can own land and businesses. **Compare and Contrast**

✓ **REVIEW ANSWER** Many Latin American countries tried to strengthen their economies through industry and manufacturing. **Main Idea and Details**

Other Nations   p. 104

- **What are some ways that science and technology have influenced the standard of living in Latin American countries?** Possible answers: Multinational companies have brought new technologies to factories in Latin America, and workers there have learned new skills to work in the factories. Industrial growth and development have helped build the economies of Latin American countries. **Cause and Effect**

✓ **REVIEW ANSWER** Latin American nations formed the Organization of American States (OAS) to provide for cooperation and peaceful settlement of conflicts. Some nations formed Mercosur to increase trade among themselves. Mexico joined NAFTA to trade freely with the United States and Canada. **Summarize**

Continuing Concerns for Latin America

p. 105

SOCIAL STUDIES STRAND
Economics

Explain to students that opportunity costs are the amounts of other goods and services that must be given up to get something else. For example, to preserve and develop rain forests, Latin American governments must give up the other uses for that land.

- **What are the opportunity costs of clearing rain forest land for agriculture?** Opportunity costs include loss of valuable rain forest plants and animals and destruction of the culture of native peoples who live there. **Evaluate**

✓ **REVIEW ANSWER** Problems facing Latin American countries include finding ways to make the best use of their resources and preserving the cultures of native peoples. ◑ **Summarize**

3 Close and Assess

Summarize the Lesson Ask students to write three questions about the material in the lesson. Then have them work in pairs to exchange questions and discuss answers.

✓ Lesson 2 REVIEW

1. ◑ **Summarize** Changes in Latin American governments gave people more rights, but economic differences among people remain a problem.

2. New laws and constitutions helped bring justice, equality, majority rule, and minority rights for Latin Americans.

3. Possible answers: The United States built and controlled the Panama Canal but turned over ownership to Panama in 1999. Mexico and the United States (and Canada) entered into the North American Free Trade Agreement.

4. The OAS resulted in stronger ties among the countries of the Americas. The International Monetary Fund (IMF) provided economic aid to help build economies in Latin America.

5. **Critical Thinking: *Analyze Information*** Developing natural resources, such as those found in rain forests, can help Latin America grow economically, but it can also harm the environment.

Link to ⌒⌒ Geography Students' reports should reflect understanding of the relationship between latitude and climate and between climate and vegetation. Students might draw maps showing where to find rain forests.

Map and Globe Skills

Discuss the causes and effects of urbanization. (People move to cities to find jobs. Cities may become overcrowded.)

Think and Apply

1. The areas of greatest growth are along the coasts or near large lakes.
2. Water is a resource important to urbanization.
3. Possible answer: Northern Canada has a harsh climate and central South America is landlocked.

READING STRATEGY
Summarize

In the Lesson Review, students complete a graphic organizer like the one below. You might want to provide students with a copy of Transparency 6 to complete as they review the lesson.

Summarize

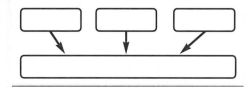

EXTEND LANGUAGE
ESL Support

Urbanization Map Terms Help students build vocabulary related to the urbanization map on p. 106.

Beginning Help students define the terms *urban* and *rural*. Have students make illustrations that demonstrate the difference in the meanings of the two terms.

Intermediate Have students demonstrate an understanding of *urban* and *rural* by writing and sharing a definition for each term.

Advanced Ask students to list activities associated with each term. For example, urban activities might include riding a subway or building a skyscraper. Discuss why each activity is suited to a rural or urban setting.

CURRICULUM CONNECTION
Science

Rain Forest Food Web
- Have students use the Internet or other library sources to find out about the plants and animals that live in a rain forest in Latin America.
- Students should use what they learn to draw a food web for the rain forest environment.
- Students can finish by writing a paragraph describing how deforestation might affect the food web.

Write the Essay

Plan and Prewrite

You may wish to have students use the documents to write an essay about how governments meet the needs of their citizens. Discuss the topic and share with students the rubric that will be used to score their essays (see TE p. 77). Have students review the documents and the answers they recorded on their DBQ Record sheets.

Page 99, photograph: Both French-speaking and English-speaking people can understand the sign.

Page 99, picture: The crown represents British Canada. The igloo, animals, and stone monument represent Inuit culture.

Page 100, chart: Oil, gases, and lumber are exports that are natural resources. Exporting these materials may help Canada's economic growth.

Page 102, photograph: She is probably new to voting because someone is helping her put her ballot in the box.

Page 104, picture: All countries in the OAS have equal status.

Page 107, interview:

- Menchú says "we indigenous peoples" because she is a Quiché Indian and wants to show that she is speaking for herself and her people.
- Menchú believes indigenous peoples need to be allowed to exist, to live, to let their culture develop, and to recover the meaning of their own history.
- Menchú says four things that can be used to protect the rights of indigenous peoples are international law, national legislation, legal protection of human rights, and the respect and acceptance of society.
- Menchú is an important spokesperson because she herself is a Quiché Indian and because she has strong feelings about what her people need and do not need.

Discuss Before students begin planning their essays, you may wish to have a class discussion to stimulate students' thinking. Ask students to identify ways governments meet the needs of their citizens. Remind students that the unit provides the historical context for their responses.

Use a Graphic Organizer Remind students that a prewriting tool such as a graphic organizer will help them write a better essay. Model on the board a word web with *Government* in the center circle of the web. Suggest that students complete the graphic organizer with information from the documents. For example, they could use the word web to brainstorm how the documents show that governments meet the needs of their citizens.

Tell students they may use other kinds of organizers, as long as the organizers are suited to the topic. Once students complete their prewriting, have them write first drafts of their essays.

Content Tips As students review the documents, encourage them to evaluate the information. Ask students why they think the governments chose to meet their citizens' needs in the manner shown in the documents.

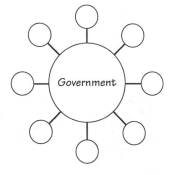

Evaluate and Revise

Check Content Once students have completed their first drafts, provide the following checklist to assist them in evaluating what they have written:

- ☐ Have I used information from the documents to draw my conclusion?
- ☐ Have I shown how information or ideas from each document are related to the topic?
- ☐ Have I included my own thoughts in the essay?
- ☐ Have I avoided simply summarizing the documents?
- ☐ Is my point clearly stated and explained?
- ☐ Is my essay logically organized?
- ☐ Do I use appropriate details to support my topic sentences?
- ☐ Have I avoided including statements that are unrelated to the topic?

Proofread After they have edited their essays for content, remind students to use a standard proofreading checklist to look for errors in spelling, grammar, and mechanics. Then have them write and submit the final drafts of their essays.

Score the Essay You may wish to use the rubric at right to score students' essays. If you have emphasized particular thinking or writing strategies during the study of Unit 9, you may wish to modify the rubric to include those skills.

Scoring Rubric
Unit 9 Document-Based Essay

4	• Shows superior understanding of the topic. • Relates each document to the topic of governments meeting the needs of their citizens. • Includes numerous insights (conclusions, inferences) that are well explained and supported by the documents. • Includes no factual or mechanical errors.
3	• Shows reasonable understanding of the topic. • Relates most of the details from the documents to the topic of governments meeting the needs of their citizens. • Includes some insights (conclusions, inferences) that are clear and for the most part supported by the documents. • Includes very few factual or mechanical errors.
2	• Shows minimal understanding of the topic. • Attempts to relate some details from the documents to the topic of governments meeting the needs of their citizens. • Includes details, quotes, or paraphrasing, but no insights (conclusions, inferences) into the topic. • Includes a number of factual or mechanical errors.
1	• Shows little or no understanding of the topic. • Does not attempt to relate details from the documents to the topic of governments meeting the needs of their citizens. • Includes only vague references, if any, to content of the documents. • Includes many factual or mechanical errors.
0	• Uses no accurate data, or response is totally unrelated to the topic. • Is either illegible or incoherent, and no sense can be made of the response. • Paper is blank.

Review

Vocabulary and People

Sample answers:

1. Pierre Trudeau was prime minister of Canada and helped pass a law that made both French and English official languages.

2. Separatism is the idea that Quebec should become a separate nation.

3. The Canada Act of 1982 ended British control over Canada's constitution.

4. Fidel Castro took over the government of Cuba in 1959 and set up a Communist government.

5. Violeta Chamorro worked to promote peace in Nicaragua.

6. The Organization of American States (OAS) promotes cultural understanding and provides for cooperation and peaceful settlement of conflicts among American nations.

7. Deforestation is the clearing of forests.

Facts and Main Ideas

Sample answers:

1. Canada created Nunavut as a homeland for the Inuit.

2. **Main Idea** Both Canada and the United States took part in World War I, World War II, the Korean War, and the Persian Gulf War. Both nations joined the United Nations, built the St. Lawrence Seaway, and joined NAFTA.

3. **Main Idea** The economies of some nations in Latin America are based mostly on industry, as are the economies of Canada and the United States.

4. Industrial growth and development has played an important role in building the economies of Latin American countries.

5. **Critical Thinking: *Compare and Contrast*** Canada and Latin American countries are concerned about how to make the best use of their natural resources. Both regions share concerns about preserving the cultures and traditions of their diverse peoples.

Write About History

1. Students' letters should reflect understanding of the traditional ways of life of the Inuit and how Nunavut provides ways to preserve their culture.

2. Students' newspaper articles should include facts about physical and human characteristics of the rain forest. They might include different points of view regarding development of rain forest resources.

3. Students' editorials should provide examples of economic decisions that affect people in Canada, the United States, and Latin America.

Read on Your Own

America's Important Neighbors: Canada, Mexico, and Cuba, by Carole Marsh (Gallopade Publishing Group, ISBN 0-635-00262-0, 2001) **Easy**

Make Your Own Inuksuk, by Mary Wallace (Owl Books, ISBN 1-894-37910-1, 2001) **Easy**

The Color of My Words, by Lynn Joseph (HarperTrophy, ISBN 0-064-47204-3, 2001) **On-Level**

Quebec (Canada in the 21st Century), by Suzanne Levert and George Sheppard (Chelsea House Publishing, ISBN 0-791-06070-5, 2001) **On-Level**

Of Kings and Fools: Stories of the French Tradition in North America, by Julien Olivier and Michael Parent (August House Publishing, ISBN 0-874-83481-3, 1996) **Challenge**

Rigoberta Menchú: Defending Human Rights in Guatemala, by Charlotte Bunch and Michael Silverstone (Feminist Press, ISBN 1-558-61199-1, 1999) **Challenge**

Index

Credits
Maps: MapQuest.com, Inc.
Photographs: Cover Corbis